EYE ON ART

Postmodern Artists
Creators of a Cultural Movement

By Amanda Vink

Portions of this book originally appeared in *Postmodern Art* by Stuart A. Kallen.

Published in 2019 by
Lucent Press, an Imprint of Greenhaven Publishing, LLC
353 3rd Avenue
Suite 255
New York, NY 10010

Designer: Deanna Paternostro
Editor: Melissa Raé Shofner

Library of Congress Cataloging-in-Publication Data

Names: Vink, Amanda, author.
Title: Postmodern artists : creators of a cultural movement / Amanda Vink.
Description: New York : Lucent Press, 2019. | Series: Eye on art | Includes
   bibliographical references and index.
Identifiers: LCCN 2018028588 (print) | LCCN 2018029121 (ebook) | ISBN
   9781534566088 (eBook) | ISBN 9781534566125 (library bound book) | ISBN
   9781534566071 (pbk. book)
Subjects: LCSH: Postmodernism–Juvenile literature.
Classification: LCC N6494.P66 (ebook) | LCC N6494.P66 V56 2019 (print) | DDC
   700/.4113–dc23
LC record available at https://lccn.loc.gov/2018028588

Printed in the United States of America

CPSIA compliance information: Batch #BW19KL: For further information contact Greenhaven Publishing LLC, New York, New York at 1-844-317-7404.

Please visit our website, www.greenhavenpublishing.com. For a free color catalog of all our high-quality
books, call toll free 1-844-317-7404 or fax 1-844-317-7405.

Contents

Foreword

What is art? There is no one answer to that question. Every person has a different idea of what makes something a work of art. Some people think of art as the work of masters such as Leonardo da Vinci, Mary Cassatt, or Michelangelo. Others see artistic beauty in everything from skyscrapers and animated films to fashion shows and graffiti. Everyone brings their own point of view to their interpretation of art.

Discovering the hard work and pure talent behind artistic techniques from different periods in history and different places around the world helps people develop an appreciation for art in all its varied forms. The stories behind great works of art and the artists who created them have fascinated people for many years and continue to do so today. Whether a person has a passion for painting, graphic design, or another creative pursuit, learning about the lives of great artists and the paths that can be taken to achieve success as an artist in the modern world can inspire budding creators to pursue their dreams.

This series introduces readers to different artistic styles, as well as the artists who made those styles famous. As they read about creative expression in the past and present, they are challenged to think critically about their own definition of art.

Quotes from artists, art historians, and other experts provide a unique perspective on each topic, and a detailed bibliography is provided as a starting place for further research. In addition, a list of websites and books about each topic encourages readers to continue their exploration of the fascinating world of art.

This world comes alive with each turn of the page, as readers explore sidebars about the artistic process and creative careers. Essential examples of different artistic styles are presented in the form of vibrant photographs and historical images, giving readers a comprehensive look at art history from ancient times to the present.

Art may be difficult to define, but it is easy to appreciate. In developing a deeper understanding of different art forms, readers will be able to look at the world around them with a fresh perspective on the beauty that can be found in unexpected places.

A Commentary on the Times

Art does not exist in a vacuum. Each artistic movement has been a reaction to both the current events of its time as well as the previous trends and movements that came before it. The artists of postmodernism, who created art between the late 1960s and the late 1990s, sought to reject the Modern Art movement that originated around 1850. To understand postmodern art, it is perhaps best to understand the elements of Modern Art that new artists threw away.

During the modern period, a few European and American artists became superstars. Painters such as Pablo Picasso, Piet Mondrian, Salvador Dalí, and Jackson Pollock were featured not only in great museums but also on the pages of popular magazines such as *LIFE* and *Look*. Young artists studied their brushstrokes, colors, and composition. Collectors desired their paintings. Actors, authors, and politicians all wanted to be seen with these artists. They were like modern rock stars, and almost everyone knew their names and their work.

Modernists created paintings that made statements and used symbolic imagery.

They, too, were rejecting art of an earlier era, specifically the painting techniques that had been valued for more than four centuries since the time of the Renaissance. The Modernists did

Artists such as Pablo Picasso rose to superstardom during the Modernist period.

away with concepts such as perspective, which gave subjects in paintings a three-dimensional, realistic look. They also refused to paint the exact likenesses of their subjects. For example, Picasso's Cubist models were shockingly portrayed with triangular eyes, misplaced noses, and shark teeth. Dalí's Surrealism was inspired by dreamlike images that, while realistic, were placed in absurd, fantastic settings. Pollock's Abstract Expressionist paintings went beyond anything ever seen before. He produced a confusion of globs, drips, and streaks of various colors, earning him the nickname Jack the Dripper.

Modernists were among a group of artists, writers, musicians, scholars, architects, and philosophers said to represent the progress and technological advancements of the 20th century. Modernists most often worked in dirty

Modernist artists were informed by their experiences with World Wars I and II, as shown here in Christopher Nevinson's Returning to the Trenches.

cities filled with trains, automobiles, airplanes, and smoke-belching factories. Their work was informed by what they had experienced, including the frightening machines of warfare that killed millions and laid the countryside to waste during World Wars I and II.

The Modernists believed their works affirmed the power of humans over machines. They also believed people could create, improve, and reshape their environment with the aid of scientific knowledge, technology, and experimentation. In their pursuit of progress, Modernists challenged every aspect of life. They wanted to advance humanity by replacing traditions they believed were standing in the way of progress.

Modernism Becomes Mainstream

At its beginning, Modern Art was seen as provocative, radical, and outrageous. To visitors at the famous Paris Salon, who were accustomed to seeing realistic works of art that closely resembled life, Modernism was quite the shock. In 1863, there were so many pieces rejected by the Salon committee that artists began to protest. Emperor Napoleon III ordered an exhibition of rejected art, which showcased work from many now-known artists such as Paul Cézanne and Édouard Manet.

Manet presented his painting *The Luncheon on the Grass*, which portrayed a nude woman having a picnic with two fully dressed males, at this show. Critics of Manet's painting commented on its skewed perspective and complained that it showed a style that was not "painterly." French art historian Ernest Chesneau remarked, "He will have talent the day that he learns how to draw and to use perspective."[1] Manet's work and the reaction to it is a fine example of the beginnings of Modernism.

However, by the mid-20th century, Modernist painters had been widely accepted. Their works were reproduced on posters and in books and magazines. Their once unique visual concepts were widely imitated by advertisers, fashion designers, and graphic artists. Modernism had become mainstream culture. Buyers eagerly purchased Modernist paintings, not for their artistic importance but for their investment value. By the late 1960s, Modernism was seen as the established order. The upcoming artists wished to distance themselves from Modernism, and so the postmodern movement was born.

Postmodern simply means "after modern," but it is often interpreted to mean anti-modern. Where Modernists hoped to discover universal truths,

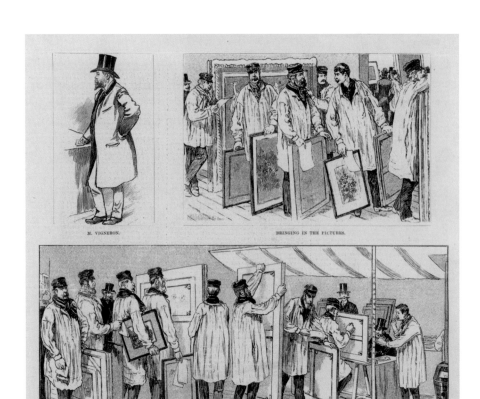

M. VIGNERON.

BRINGING IN THE PICTURES.

BRINGING IN THE PICTURES: MEASURING, NUMBERING, AND INSCRIBING.

A CONSPICUOUS YOUNG ARTIST.

LATE ARRIVALS.

FINISHING TOUCHES.

These sketches from the Illustrated London News *in 1887 show the Paris Salon, the official art exhibition of the French Academy of Fine Arts.*

postmodernists aimed to challenge them. Postmodern artists combined any and every visual style, and they embraced so-called low art forms such as commercials, magazines, and graphic arts. They saw stark artistic beauty in trash or industrial waste, which became known as "found art." The modern televised media also provided inspiration with its nonstop barrage of incongruent and disconnected images. As such, a postmodern piece might include words from an ad, images from the Renaissance, garbage found in a gutter, and a bank of video monitors showing contrasting images. With a wide variety of tools and images, postmodernists were free to combine any elements or styles in a piece. They could also use their work to make humorous, ironic, satirical, or playful statements.

The term "postmodern" can be difficult to define. The differences between Modernism and postmodernism are often razor-thin. As the late poet and art critic David Antin noted, "From the modernism you choose, you get the postmodernism you deserve."[2] Indeed, one must focus on the theory that went into a piece of art to notice the difference. The Tate Gallery, an art museum in London, England, notes on its website that in postmodernist terms, "interpretation of our experience was more concrete than abstract principles."[3]

"High Art" Versus "Low Art"

One of the important hallmarks of postmodern art is how it rejects the Modernist view of art as a serious endeavor. Modernism put the top artists on a pedestal. The suggestion was that "high art" could only be made by a talented and professional few. Postmodernism, however, argued that art could be anything, and it could be made by anyone. By doing so, postmodernists liberated arts and artists, but they also generated a fair share of criticism. As photographer and critic David Bates noted, "For the cultural conservatives, postmodern culture was [seen as] destroying the important distinctions within society about what was good culture (classical music, theatre, painting, novels) and what was not (pop, television, photography and video, tabloids and celebrity magazines)."[4]

Some argue this breakdown between old concepts and new is a result of the television and digital age. Most postmodern artists were of the first television generation, baby boomers who grew up watching TV. As children, they viewed gruesome images of the Vietnam War on the evening news mixed with commercials for shiny new cars and gleaming kitchen appliances. While most people considered these jumbled images a normal part of daily life, postmodernists viewed them as absurd. They found similarly ridiculous situations and images everywhere in modern culture. Homeless people slept in the streets beneath luminous skyscrapers; wealthy, educated businessmen cheated the public with limitless greed; and corrupt politicians lectured the public about law and order.

Rather than trying to make sense of this senseless world, postmodernists depicted the absurd through art. In this way, they called attention to the mindless messages of the media and attempted to remove society's blinders.

Postmodernism dominated the art world until the rise of the digital age in the 21st century. Even though postmodern artists did not follow any set rules, their impact on art and media in today's world is apparent. Many artists of today combine a variety of styles and mediums, and the definition of art is now open to any style and any topic.

CHAPTER ONE

From Modern to Postmodern

Current events are a huge influence for artists. Art critics set the beginning of the postmodern movement in the late 1960s, a time of civil rights advocacy, environmentalism, and the Vietnam War. It was a time of great divide between older and younger generations. Millions of young people rejected the morals of their parents, and new artists rejected the value of a modern technological society.

However, artists also gathered their inspiration from things that had come before. Artists took the inspiration they liked, and they left out what they did not like. Without Modernism, there would be no postmodernism. Thus, it is important to understand some of the artists whose work directly influenced the postmodernists.

Influence

Postmodern artists combined several types of art into one genre, or style. They constructed pictures by gluing pieces of cloth, newspaper, written words, photographs, and other objects to the surface of a painting, a technique known as collage or montage. They assembled found objects such as trash, clothing, and household items into assemblage art. They used dance, music, theatrics, and newer forms of media, such as computers, in performance art. They also used pranks and humor to mock or criticize popular culture, politics, and social traditions. Some of these facets of postmodern art, however, are not unique, and in fact, their roots can be traced to Pablo Picasso.

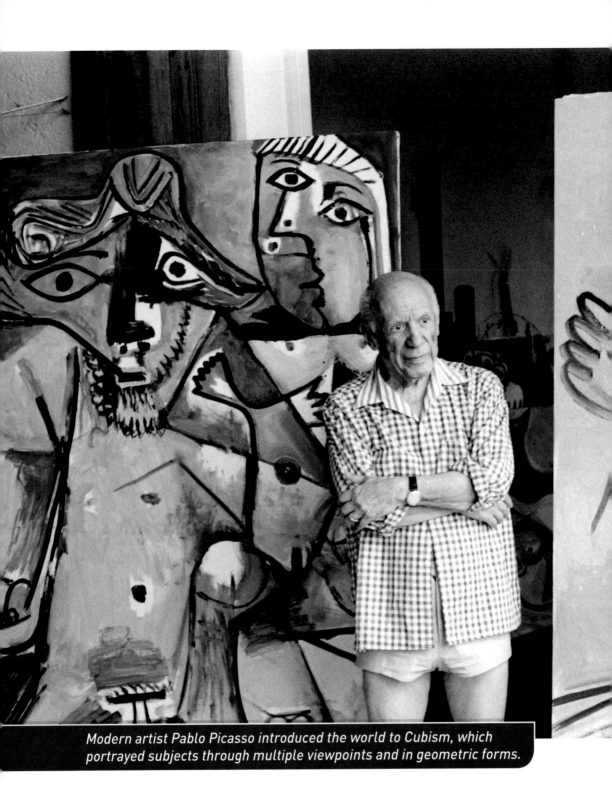

Modern artist Pablo Picasso introduced the world to Cubism, which portrayed subjects through multiple viewpoints and in geometric forms.

In the spring of 1907, Picasso began work on the revolutionary painting *The Young Ladies of Avignon*. In the painting, Picasso depicted his female models in distorted perspective with uneven angles in chunky blocks. It was the birth of the style of Cubism. Picasso was inspired by the angular faces carved in ancient African ceremonial masks.

Some believe Picasso was the first to use collage in a work of art. In 1912, he made *Still Life with Chair Caning* by pasting a piece of printed oilcloth that resembled woven chair caning onto a canvas. He added the letters "JOU" (a pun on the French word for "play") cut from the masthead of the French newspaper *Le Journal*. Finally, he framed the entire oval-shaped picture with a piece of rope.

Picasso also created the first of what is now called constructed sculpture. *Guitar* is an angular, Cubist version of a guitar made from sheet metal and wire. Unlike any other previous sculpture, *Guitar* was not cast from metal or carved from a single block of wood or stone. Instead, it was assembled out of separate elements. This work opened the door for the

20th-century constructed sculpture and assemblage movements.

A Step Further

While Picasso was experimenting with Cubism and other visual styles, the French artist Marcel Duchamp was also creating ripples in the art world, though in entirely different ways. In 1912, Duchamp painted the Cubist masterpiece *Nude Descending a Staircase, No. 2*. Going beyond Picasso's flat, motionless images, Duchamp portrayed an abstract figure in a series of images overlaid or superimposed over one another. Inspired by stop-motion photography, a medium that was popular at the time, Duchamp's distorted figures give the impression of movement.

While Duchamp had hoped to debut his work in the Salon des Indépendants's exhibition of Cubist work, he was shocked when the painting was rejected. The hanging committee—including the artist's two brothers, Jacques Villon and Raymond Duchamp-Villon—argued, "A nude never descends the stairs—a nude reclines."[5] When Duchamp submitted *Nude Descending a Staircase, No. 2* to the 1913 Armory Show in New York City, it created a scandal. Americans were accustomed to realistic art and had little exposure to the European Cubist phenomenon. An art critic for the *New York Times* wrote that the painting resembled an "explosion in a shingle factory."[6] Stung by this experience, Duchamp criticized the idea of artistic genres and ideals of beauty. After visiting an aviation exhibition and viewing airplanes, he told his friend, Romanian sculptor Constantin Brancusi, "Painting's washed up. Who'll do anything better than that propeller?"[7]

In the pursuit of mechanical beauty, Duchamp combined everyday objects into an unusual work of art. He drilled a hole in the seat of a plain white wooden stool and attached a bicycle wheel on its front fork. Commenting on the pleasure he received from spinning the wheel, Duchamp later said, "I enjoyed looking at it, just as I enjoy looking at the flames dancing in a fireplace."[8]

When World War I began in 1914, Duchamp moved to New York City in 1915 to avoid being drafted into the French army. Much to the artist's surprise, he found that he had become a celebrity due to the *Nude Descending a Staircase, No. 2* controversy. When he showed *Bicycle Wheel* to several art patrons, they named the individual parts of the work "readymades." This name could apply to any object the artist purchased "as a sculpture already made." When Duchamp modified these objects, for example, by mounting the wheel on the stool, he called them "assisted readymades."[9]

Although they were created in a spirit of playful humor, Duchamp's readymades challenged basic concepts of art. Throughout history,

Marcel Duchamp (shown here) became a celebrity after he submitted *Nude Descending a Staircase, No. 2* to the 1913 Armory Show in New York City. He was a major influence for postmodern artists.

Everyday Objects As Art

M arcel Duchamp displayed everyday objects as works of art called readymades. The Museum of Modern Art (MoMA) explained the concepts behind his work *Bicycle Wheel*:

> Bicycle Wheel *is Duchamp's first Readymade, a class of artworks that raised fundamental questions about artmaking and, in fact, about art's very definition ... Duchamp was not the first to kidnap everyday stuff for art; the Cubists had done so in collages, which, however, required aesthetic judgment in the shaping and placing of materials. The Readymade, on the other hand, implied that the production of art need be no more than a matter of selection—of choosing a preexisting object. In radically subverting earlier assumptions about what the artmaking process entailed, this idea had enormous influence on later artists, particularly ... in the 1950s and 1960s.*
>
> *The components of* Bicycle Wheel, *being mass-produced, are anonymous, identical or similar to countless others. In addition, the fact that this version of the piece is not the original seems inconsequential, at least in terms of visual experience. Duchamp claimed to like the work's appearance, "to feel that the wheel turning was very soothing." Even now,* Bicycle Wheel *retains an absurdist visual surprise.*[1]

1. Museum of Modern Art, *MOMA Highlights: 350 Works from the Museum of Modern Art*. New York, NY: Museum of Modern Art, 2004, p. 87.

artists were expected to possess uncommon talent and skill. When Duchamp bolted a bicycle wheel onto a stool and called it art, he made a statement that anything could be art if it was displayed as such. This rejection of art came to be called anti-art. It required the creator to build the work. It did not require a preconceived vision, artistic inspiration, or sense of aesthetics (or an appreciation of art or beauty). As Duchamp said, "You have to approach something with an indifference, as if you have no aesthetic emotion. The choice of readymades is always based on visual indifference and, at the same time, on the total absence of good or bad taste."[10]

A Rivalry

The differences in the theory behind Picasso's and Duchamp's work were enormous. Picasso's focus was on the piece of art itself. He said, "When I paint my object is to show what I have found and not what I am looking for. In art intentions are not sufficient and, as we say in Spanish: love must be proved by facts and not by reasons."[11] In stark contrast, Duchamp's method was the exact opposite. He said, "I was interested in ideas, not in visual products. I wanted to put painting again in the service of the mind."[12] To Duchamp, the idea behind a piece of work was more important than what was represented. He is considered by many to be the father of Conceptual art.

Although Picasso and Duchamp shared both social circles and even collectors, they were rivals. However, in spite of their different opinions on the process of creating art, both Picasso and Duchamp had an extreme effect on the postmodern movement. It may come as little surprise that the postmodernists championed Duchamp, whose emphasis was not on the art itself.

Picasso was unable to reconcile Duchamp's success. According to Picasso's biographer John Richardson, "If it had been Matisse, who was always a rival, it wouldn't have mattered. But who were they looking up to on the other side of the Atlantic but Marcel Duchamp of all people! Picasso despised him."[13] In fact, when Duchamp passed away, Picasso's only comment was allegedly, "He was wrong."[14]

Making Manifestos

Manifestos, or a public declaration of intentions and motives, were very popular during both the Modernist and postmodernist movements. Manifestos represent ideologies, and in many cases, they are written to convince others to follow suit. Artistic manifestos really took off after the publication of F. T. Marinetti's first Futurist manifesto in 1909. Originating in Italy, Futurism was a style of art that was passionate in its resolve to condemn the past. It was speed and movement that the Futurists sought. They wanted to get as far away from the past as possible, by any means necessary. "The sensation of velocity and momentum by men, beasts and machines are to be celebrated and consummated in towering acts of aggression and destruction,"[15] explained journalist Robert Fox in a 2009 article.

Tricked by the Media

Another group of artists—the Dadaists—were creating anti-art on their own terms. Dadaism began in Zurich, Switzerland, in 1916 during the bloody and senseless destruction of World War I. Dadaists believed the unprecedented slaughter was a result of a society that worshiped machines and technology. They believed this misplaced respect for science and industry resulted in the horrors of mechanized warfare— tanks, machine guns, poison gas, and hand grenades.

Dadaists believed that the pillars of society, such as law, faith,

F. T. Marinetti, shown here, sparked the Futurist art movement in 1909 when he published his first Futurist manifesto.

language, economy, education, and traditional gender roles, had failed to prevent the unprecedented destruction of the war. They also held that society had been tricked into this illogical behavior by a new form of communication: mass media. Leah Dickerman of the Museum of Modern Art (MoMA) explained in *Dada*:

Propaganda poster campaigns

with coordinated messages were deployed on a massive scale. The development of communication technology— radio, cinema, and newsreels, and a new photo-illustrated press— fostered the flow of information from battlefront to home front. The science of wireless telegraphy ... led to a surge in public broadcasting and the mass production of "radio music boxes" in its wake. Newsreels, which first appeared in 1911, captured battle action ... and nurtured the emergence of a commercial film industry ... These wartime developments triggered a postwar massmedia explosion ... For the individual observer, there was a threshold jump in the number of images and amount of print material circulated in the public sphere.[16]

Artistic Anarchy

Dadaists utilized new communication methods to express their loss of faith in society. The German poet Hugo Ball, founder of the Dada movement, believed reason, logic, and science led to the insanity of war. He argued the only sane reaction was to throw those lines of thinking aside. Instead, he promoted artistic anarchy with irrational statements and illogical anti-art. Early Dada poet Tristan Tzara described his view of the movement: "The beginnings of Dada were not the beginnings of an art, but those of a disgust."[17]

Switzerland was neutral during the war, and many painters, poets, and performers fled to Zurich to avoid the bloodshed. Ball saw an opportunity to bring these like-minded young artists and war resisters together. In February 1916, he opened a nightclub called the Cabaret Voltaire. Within a week, it was filled with a group of nonconformists who formed the core of the Dada movement. They included Tzara; Ball's wife, poet, singer, and dancer Emily Hennings; French-German sculptor and painter Jean (Hans) Arp; and German poet, writer, and drummer Richard Huelsenbeck.

Arp created two of the earliest Dada works of art, *According to the Laws of Chance* and *Untitled (Collage with Squares Arranged According to the Law of Chance)*. As the titles suggest, Arp composed these collages by chance. He dropped torn bits of paper

The Dada Manifesto

On July 14, 1916, the German poet Hugo Ball released "The Dada Manifesto," which explained in abstract and somewhat confusing terms the Dada movement he helped invent:

> Dada is a new tendency in art ... Dada comes from the dictionary. It is terribly simple. In French it means "hobby horse." In German it means "good-by," "Get off my back," "Be seeing you sometime." In Romanian: "Yes, indeed, you are right, that's it. But of course, yes, definitely, right." And so forth...
>
> How does one achieve eternal bliss? By saying dada. How does one become famous? By saying dada. With a noble gesture and delicate propriety. Till one goes crazy. Till one loses consciousness. How can one get rid of everything that [smacks] of journalism, worms, everything nice and right, blinkered, moralistic, Europeanized, enervated?
>
> By saying dada. Dada is the world soul, dada is the pawnshop. Dada is the world's best lily-milk soap ...
>
> I don't want words that other people have invented. All the words are other people's inventions. I want my own stuff, my own rhythm, and vowels and consonants too, matching the rhythm and all my own.[1]

1. Hugo Ball, "Dada Manifesto," 391.org, July 14, 1916. www.391.org/manifestos/hugoball_dadamanifesto.htm.

onto the floor in a random method and pasted them onto a piece of paper more or less as they had fallen. As explained on the MoMA website,

This elegantly composed collage of torn-and-pasted paper is a playful, almost syncopated [musically rhythmic] composition in which uneven squares seem to dance within the space ... Arp [developed this] method of making collages ... in order to create a work that was free of human intervention and closer to nature. The incorporation of chance operations was a way of removing the artist's will from the creative act ... so as to divorce his work from [what Arp called] "the life of the hand."[18]

Arp's work inspired German poet, painter, sculptor, and collage artist Kurt Schwitters in Hanover, Germany. Schwitters's first collage,

Hugo Ball, founder of the Dada movement, is shown here in 1916 reciting poetry at the Cabaret Voltaire while wearing a homemade suit.

Hansi, strongly resembles Arp's work. Soon after, however, he began to follow his own path. He made assemblages from scraps of found materials, which included tram tickets, coupons, postage stamps, beer labels, candy wrappers, newspaper clippings, fabric swatches, and rusty nails. Schwitters felt that these items reflected the flux, or changeability, of modern society. Schwitters called one collage a Merz picture, and afterward, referred to all his work as Merz, which he said meant "a principle of openness toward everything."[19] One such piece, *Merz Column*, consists of a square column covered with words and images from newspapers and magazines. Various items sit atop the column, including a baby-doll head, a cow horn, a laurel branch, some crocheted cloth, and various items made from plaster, metal, and wood.

"The Poem Will Be Like You"

Schwitters was also a poet who used collage methods to construct poems, putting together random words to create a single piece. Tzara, who pioneered this technique, explained that to write Dada poetry an artist should:

Take a newspaper.
Take a pair of scissors.
Choose an article …
Cut out the article.
Then cut out each of the words
that make up this article
and put them in a bag.
Shake it gently.
Then take out the scraps one
after the other in the order
in which they left the bag.
Copy [onto paper] …
The poem will be like you.[20]

Ball used Tzara's technique to create his 1916 manifesto, which introduced the Dada philosophy to a mass audience. By stringing together seemingly incongruous phrases, made-up words, and poetic symbols, "The Dada Manifesto" makes three main points:

1. *Dada is international in perspective and seeks to bridge differences.*
2. *Dada is antagonistic toward established society … and*
3. *Dada is a new tendency in art that seeks to change conventional attitudes and practices in aesthetics, society, and morality.*[21]

Ball also published several magazines with Dada poetry and art. Meanwhile, Tzara was producing his own Dada poems and manifestos. One of his books, with the unusual title *The First Celestial Adventure of Mr. Antipyrine, Fire Extinguisher*, was a script from a performance piece given at the Cabaret Voltaire. This book, with characters named

Mr. Antipyrine, Fire Extinguisher, and Mr. Shriekshriek, was sent to Duchamp in New York. It was the first time the readymade artist saw the word *Dada*. Although Duchamp is today associated with the founding of Dadaism, he insisted for many years that the crowd in Zurich did not influence him: "It was parallel, if you wish … [My work] wasn't Dada, but it was in the same spirit, without, however, being in the Zurich spirit."[22]

Fountain

Despite his denials, Duchamp is forever associated with Dada due to his readymade piece *Fountain*. The work is a urinal the artist bought at a plumbing supply store, J. L. Mott Iron Works, on Fifth Avenue in New York City. Duchamp took the urinal to his studio, turned it 90 degrees from its normal position, so the rounded front jutted up into the air, and wrote "R. Mutt 1917" on its side.

Duchamp was a board member of the Society of Independent Artists. He entered *Fountain* in its first annual exhibition in April 1917, under the pseudonym R. Mutt. Although the group's policy was to display any artwork submitted, it refused to put *Fountain* in the show. Some board members believed it was immoral and vulgar, while others said it was plagiarism since it was a plain piece of plumbing. A response to these charges, thought to be written by Duchamp, appeared in the Dada magazine *Blind Man*:

Now Mr. Mutt's fountain is not immoral, that is absurd … It is a fixture which you see every day in plumbers' show windows.

Whether Mr. Mutt made the fountain with his own hands or not has no importance. He CHOSE it. He took an article of life, placed it so that its useful significance disappeared under the new title and point of view—created a new thought for that object.

As for plumbing, that is absurd. The only works of art America has produced are her plumbing and her bridges.[23]

The rejection of *Fountain* caused a sensation covered extensively by the New York press. The widespread shock and controversy became part of the Dada joke. By its overreaction to the sight of a common plumbing fixture, society was made to look ridiculous, much more so than the artist who attempted to display it.

Duchamp continued in the Dadaist spirit of revolt against art and morality. In 1919, he created *L.H.O.O.Q.* by drawing facial hair on a small, cheap reproduction of one of the world's most admired paintings: the *Mona Lisa* by Leonardo da Vinci. According to the Duchamp World Community

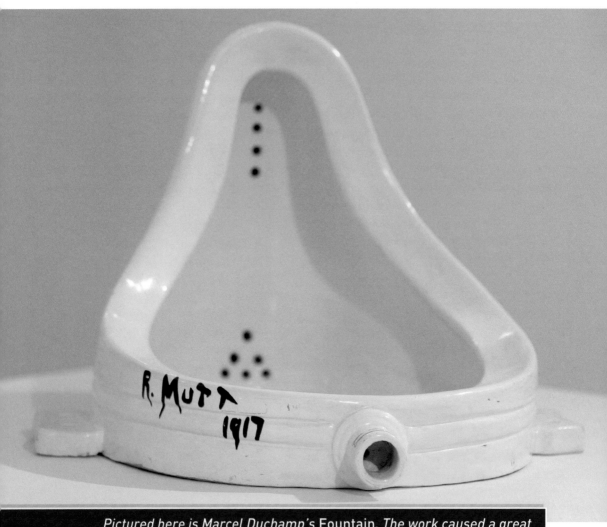

Pictured here is Marcel Duchamp's **Fountain**. *The work caused a great stir in the art community when it was rejected for a 1917 exhibition put on by the Society of Independent Artists. The original work was lost, but copies of it still exist.*

website, "The 'readymade' … is one of the most well known [acts] of degrading a famous work of art."[24]

After Dada

By the early 1920s, many Dadaists moved on to other art movements. In Paris, France, Dadaist André Breton felt the movement was at turns either too scathing and negative or too silly, what he called "Dada Buffoonery."[25] Breton began promoting a new style called Surrealism. This art concept was based on dreamlike images that

Being in the Painting

On August 8, 1949, *LIFE* magazine ran an article on Jackson Pollock along with photos of him at work. The article, "Is He the Greatest Living Painter in the United States?," is excerpted below:

"When I am in my painting," says Pollock, "I'm not aware of what I'm doing." To find out what he has been doing he stops and contemplates the picture during what he calls his "get acquainted" period. Once in a while a lifelike image appears in the painting by mistake. But Pollock cheerfully rubs it out because the picture must retain "a life of its own." Finally, after days of brooding and doodling, Pollock decides the painting is finished, a deduction few others are equipped to make. [1]

1. Quoted in "Jackson Pollock: Is He the Greatest Living Painter in the United States?," *LIFE*, August 8, 1949, p. 45.

ran through Breton's mind in the moments before falling asleep. The images might be of realistic, common objects, but they were viewed in absurd, otherworldly settings. Spanish artist Salvador Dalí created some of the most famous Surrealist imagery. In one work, he painted melted watches draped over tree branches. In another, he painted disjointed body parts in barren landscapes.

Although the Dada era was over, the style influenced a generation of American artists who began their careers after World War II at the height of the Modernist movement. Foremost among them was Wyoming-born painter Jackson Pollock, who created what came to be called "action paintings" for the ferocious dance the artist performed to create them. Pollock began a work by tacking a large piece of unframed canvas to the floor. Picking up buckets of thick liquid paint called gloss enamel, he danced and jumped around the canvas. He either poured various colors onto the medium or dripped and splashed the paint with sticks, trowels, knives, hardened brushes, and turkey basters. As it dried, he deliberately added sand, broken glass, nails, coins, and even cigarette butts to the sticky paint.

Pollock's manner of action painting was based on what Dadaists and Surrealists called automatism. This theory supposes that artists can create works based on unconscious thoughts, revelations, and moods rather than through a planned process.

Pollock's drip paintings created a sensation, and the artist was featured in a number of popular magazines.

Jackson Pollock had no plans for his paintings. What was left on each canvas was the result of his movements around the room.

Although Pollock disdained such publicity, it is clear he redefined how artwork was created. His move away from the easel, brush, and palette liberated artists from any and all artistic traditions. Pollock also presented a romantic view of the artist as someone who was defined by his work and believed that painting was a way of life.

The Three Types of Abstract Expressionism

Pollock belonged to what was called the New York School of painters. (In this usage, "school" is not a learning institution but is used to define a group of people who share a similar artistic philosophy and style.) Their work came to be known as Abstract Expressionism, and in addition to Pollock, other Abstract Expressionists include Willem de Kooning, Franz Kline, and Mark Rothko. These painters are categorized into two groups. Some, such as Rothko, are called color field artists because they painted simple, unified blocks of color onto a canvas. Others, such as Pollock and de Kooning, are called action painters who used automatic art techniques to create abstract works with no definable subject matter.

A third type of Abstract Expressionism is seen in the works of Texas-born artist Robert Rauschenberg. In the 1950s, Rauschenberg created a series of works, called "combines," that blended abstract artwork with various objects. These pieces of assemblage art, created from preserved animals, large objects, and commercial photography, are reminiscent of works by Schwitters. For example, the unusual materials in a Rauschenberg piece called *Untitled*, created in 1954, are described by New York's Metropolitan Museum of Art as "oil, pencil, crayon, paper, canvas, fabric, newspaper, photographs, wood, glass, mirror, tin, cork and found painting with pair of painted leather shoes, dried grass, and Dominique hen mounted on wood structure on five casters."[26]

These artists are of a movement known as late Modernist art. While artists had begun to throw away some of the ideas of Modernism—the value of a completed piece, for example—they had not yet crossed over the line into postmodernism.

"The Meaning May Just Be That the Painting Exists"

By the mid-1950s, New York artists were searching for a style to follow Abstract Expressionism. Jasper Johns believed he found an answer. He began creating paintings with familiar images such as words, numbers, and flags. He created the piece called *White Flag* in 1955, which was an American flag constructed from tinted beeswax (called encaustic), newsprint, fabric, and charcoal.

In the years that followed, Johns created several more American flags.

The painting on the left, a 1952 piece called Blue Poles, is an example of Pollock's style.

He also created works containing targets, numbers, letters, maps, rulers, beer cans, and puzzle pieces. Like Pollock, Johns believed the act of creation was as important as the work of art itself. Regarding the simplicity of the subject matter, Johns stated, "There may or may not be an idea, and the meaning may just be that the painting exists."[27]

In the early 1960s, artists David Hockney, Richard Hamilton, and Roy Lichtenstein took the idea of using familiar images one step further. Using images drawn from popular mass culture, these artists created Popular Art, or Pop Art. These images were meant to have a broader appeal than the academic and obscure images of the Abstract Expressionists. Hamilton's early work features abstract images of American automobiles, while Lichtenstein painted giant cartoons similar to those found in comic books.

Hockney created images based on his travels to

Los Angeles, California, in the 1960s. For example, *A Bigger Splash* shows in simple geometric patterns a diving board, a swimming pool, a typical California ranch house, and two palm trees. Bright blue dominates the painting in the pool and the sky. The color was applied in several layers with a paint roller typically used for painting walls.

Andy Warhol and Pop Art

Andy Warhol was a commercial artist in New York City in 1962 when a friend suggested he make a painting of something very common, something everyone would recognize, "like a can of Campbell's soup."[28] A few months later, Warhol displayed 32 oversized, realistic paintings of Campbell's soup cans in a Los Angeles gallery. Some canvases featured a single can. Others had 100 cans of different flavors, such as black bean, bean and bacon, and vegetable. Critics panned the show for its lack of originality, while the supermarket near the gallery stacked real cans of Campbell's soup in the window, offering to sell the real item that inspired the artwork for 29 cents a can. Despite the scorn and negative reviews, the publicity made Warhol an international Pop Art sensation.

After achieving instant fame, Warhol set up an art studio in New York and named it "the Factory." As the name implies, he used the Factory to mass-produce art. Abandoning paintbrushes, he created silk-screen portraits of famous people such as actress Marilyn Monroe, former first lady Jackie Kennedy, and Chinese dictator Mao Zedong. He even created

Andy Warhol became the most famous Pop artist after he began to mass-produce images out of his New York studio called the Factory.

self-portraits using his signature style of brightly colored repeated images. According to the MoMA website, "Engaging in the painting of self-portraits only further cultivated his fame. In time, Warhol's self-portraits became as famous as the iconic portraits of Marilyn Monroe or [actress] Elizabeth Taylor. The artist had himself become a celebrity."[29]

Using silk screening allowed Warhol to mass-produce images on an unprecedented scale. He embraced commercialism and did not attribute an ideal or meaning to his work. As a result, he became the biggest name in Pop Art. Some art scholars view the first Pop Art exhibits as postmodern, but the term postmodernism was not dominant until afterward. Pop Art was important, however, in that it cleared the divide between high art and low art, which paved the way for postmodernism.

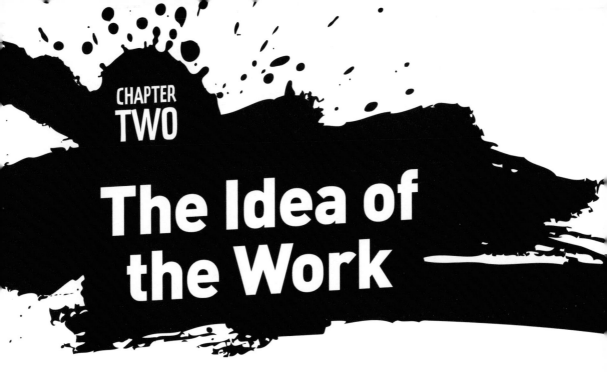

The Idea of the Work

M odernist art was not always easy for viewers to understand. The result was an industry that was successful because its job was to dissect art and explain it to the public. The role of the critic became important. However, artists continued to follow their vision, keeping their intentions to themselves and leaving the analysis to others.

The relationship between artist and critic began to break down in the late 1950s with the advent of Conceptual art. Rather than let a middleman, such as a critic, define art for the public, the Conceptual artist explained their ideas with words or written instructions. While these, too, were often baffling, the concepts and intentions defined by the artist came to play an important role in the total artwork. Conceptual art is considered one of the first full-blown movements that can be labeled postmodernism.

Anyone Can Make Art

American Conceptual artist Sol LeWitt conceived of more than 1,200 large wall paintings that were executed by others who used his artistic statements to create the works. His paintings featured geometric designs such as stars, rectangles, and stripes. Some were drab and neutral, while others were bursting with color. The directions to *Wall Drawing 766* give insight into LeWitt's work. He provided vague directions to draftspersons and painters, stating simply, "Twenty-one isometric cubes of varying sizes each with color ink

Looks Are Not Important

In 1967, Sol LeWitt described his work in an *Artforum* article titled "Paragraphs on Conceptual Art," excerpted below:

I will refer to the kind of art in which I am involved as conceptual art ... This kind of art is not theoretical or illustrative of theories; it is intuitive [instinctive and spontaneous], it is involved with all types of mental processes and it is purposeless. It is usually free from the dependence on the skill of the artist as a craftsman. It is the objective of the [conceptual] artist ... to make his work mentally interesting to the spectator, and therefore usually he would want it to become emotionally dry. There is no reason to suppose, however, that the conceptual artist is out to bore the viewer ...

What the work of art looks like isn't too important. It has to look like something if it has physical form. No matter what form it may finally have it must begin with an idea.[1]

1. Sol LeWitt, "Paragraphs on Conceptual Art," *Artforum*, June 1967. www.corner-college. com/udb/cproVozeFxParagraphs_on_Conceptual_Art._Sol_leWitt.pdf.

washes superimposed."[30]

Postmodernism calls into question the way things had been traditionally executed. In the case of LeWitt, he may have been questioning the role of the artist. In this viewer-constructed exhibit, LeWitt may have been asking, *who is the artist?* Also, *how important is the artist?* Melissa Ho, former assistant curator at the Hirschhorn Museum, gives a possible explanation. "In this post-war generation," she said, "there is this trend, in a way, toward democratizing art ... it is this opinion that anyone can make art."[31]

While the idea of assembling someone else's art piece may sound dry and uninteresting, when *Wall Drawing 766* was recreated on the walls of the Whitney Museum of American Art in New York in 2000, the colorful, mural-sized concept took teams of painters and designers weeks to finish. LeWitt believed that the hazy instruction inspired joy, frustration, boredom, or nervousness on the part of the painters. These emotions became as important as the finished work of art itself.

LeWitt's painting conformed to another aspect of Conceptual art. Because of its placement on a wall in the Whitney, *Wall Drawing 766* was eventually painted over. Therefore, the concept left no lasting object of monetary value, an idea valued by Conceptual artists.

LeWitt, explaining the theory

behind his wall paintings, said, "In conceptual art the idea or concept is the most important aspect of the work ... all of the planning and decisions are made beforehand and the execution is a perfunctory [unthinking] affair. The idea becomes a machine that makes the art."[32]

"Demolish Serious Culture!"

In its simplest form, the word "concept" means "an idea of what something is or how it works."[33] Ideas and notions form the basis of Conceptual art. However, the term has also been used to challenge basic notions of Modernism, in which physical materials (paint and canvas) are used to create an art object, such as a painting.

In 1961, anti-art activist Henry Flynt rejected notions of physical art objects when he coined the term "concept art:" "Concept art is ... an art of which the material is *concepts*, as the material of ... music is sound. Since concepts are closely bound up with language, concept art is a kind of art of which the material is language."[34] By claiming that Conceptual artists no longer needed to master paint and brush, but only words and ideas, Flynt questioned the very nature of who is—or is not—an artist. This was seen as a postmodernist concept because it challenged the very nature of what was or was not art.

Conceptual artists also rebelled against the power of the art establishment, which controlled the art world through galleries and museums. The establishment included art agents who promoted favored artists and trends, writers and critics for art magazines, and art historians and collectors. This loose organization of powerful, often wealthy, art lovers could make someone such as Pollock famous overnight or punish a new talent if they were seen as unfashionable or too strange.

Conceptualists decided to make art that could not be marketed and sold as a commodity or a commercial product. Instead, these artists focused on the concepts behind a piece of work. In doing so, they subverted, or undermined the authority of, the traditional art market. Suddenly, art galleries and museums lost their esteem and power as they could no longer influence their will over buyers and distributors of art. According to Conceptual artist Daniel Buren, this created a widespread fear of Conceptualism: "Panic strikes the art establishment as its members begin to realize that the very foundation on which their power is established—art itself—is about to disappear."[35]

Flynt used humor to make fun of so-called "serious" art. He organized small picket lines around art museums and concerts, carrying satirical signs that read "No More Art!" and "Demolish Serious Culture!"

Klein's Challenges

While Flynt used wit as a weapon against the art world, pioneering French artist Yves Klein used performance to confront, attack, and offend the establishment. Klein's first challenge to the art world occurred in 1958 when he held the exhibit *The Void* at the Iris Clert Gallery in Paris. Klein created a void, meaning empty space or something of no consequence, in preparation for the event. He painted the entire room white, then said he created immaterial, or imaginary, paintings.

On the night of the exhibition, Klein seated himself in the middle of the empty gallery. He had sent out a large number of invitations, and by 10 p.m., about 3,000 people were packed into the narrow street in front of the gallery. Police and fire trucks had to be called to disperse the crowd. Inside, Klein, who now called himself the Painter of Space, sold several immaterial paintings to amused buyers after bargaining shrewdly over the price. Commenting on the meaning of Klein's concept in *The Triumph of Anti-Art*, the late professor and art critic Thomas McEvilley wrote, "*The Void* was a derisive [mocking] critique of the art object, the art business, and the role of the artist."[36]

One of Klein's most controversial pieces was called *Anthropométries of the Blue Epoch*. The artist directed the creation of work without ever touching the materials. At the public event, held in a gallery, a string ensemble played *Monotone-Silence Symphony*, written by Klein. The song consisted of one chord, a D-major, played for 20 minutes, followed by an equal period of silence. Artwork was created by women who applied blue paint, called International Klein Blue, to their nude bodies. At the instruction of the artist, the women rolled around on large sheets of paper. In this manner, Klein produced 200 body paintings, or anthropometries, made with "living paintbrushes."[37] These works were viewed as parodies of traditional figure paintings in which artists painted nude models.

Unconventional Art Spaces

Klein died of a heart attack at the age of 34. At the time of his death in 1962, many Europeans considered him the most important French artist since World War II. However, many Conceptualists had moved away from the idea of an art gallery as an exhibition space even for Conceptual art. Now, they were enacting art concepts on the streets, out in the open and among average people.

In 1962, fascinated by measurement and direction, Stanley Brouwn walked cities and counted his steps. He asked pedestrians for directions, and he asked them to draw maps to various places. He asked them for the number of footsteps it would take to get to his destination. When they did not draw him anything, he presented blank sheets of paper. This project became

This Way Brouwn. By 1969, he had collected 500 such maps, which he displayed in an exhibit. These pieces were meant to demonstrate the ways in which people perceive and measure urban space.

Throughout his life, Brouwn adamantly refused to be interviewed or photographed. He also refused to let his work be reproduced. Brouwn's silence allowed the work to speak for itself without it being colored by statements from the artist.

The idea of using city streets for art was taken in a different direction by Bulgarian-born American artist Christo and his French wife Jeanne-Claude. In 1958, Christo developed the concept of drawing attention to an object by hiding it. To do so, Christo wrapped everyday objects—such as a wine bottle, a pile of magazines, a nightstand, a motorcycle, and even a Volkswagen car—in sheets of fabric. By hiding an object, it became a piece of art worthy of consideration and study.

In 1961, Christo and Jeanne-Claude applied this idea of "wrapping" to outdoor artworks called *Stacked Oil Barrels* and *Dockside Packages* at Cologne Harbor on the Rhine River in Germany. Christo and Jeanne-Claude borrowed materials from the dockworkers and wrapped tarps around a stack of oil barrels, securing them with rope. At the same site, they wrapped packages at the dockside with tarps. These works stood for two weeks and then were dismantled.

Temporary Monuments

Artists Christo and Jeanne-Claude were famous for wrapping buildings and parks in plastic and canvas and creating what they called "temporary monuments." In an interview posted on the *Journal of Contemporary Art* website, Christo explained their concepts of space and art:

> *Everything in the world is owned by somebody: somebody designed the sidewalks, or the streets, even the highway, somebody even designed the airways. [Twenty-four] hours around the clock, we move in a highly precise space designed by politicians, urban planners, and of course that space is full of regulations, ownerships, jurisdictions, meanings. I love that space. We go in that space and we create gentle disturbances in that space. Basically, we are borrowing that space and use it intricately for a short time.*[1]

1. Quoted in Gianfranco Mantegna, "Christo and Jeanne-Claude," *Journal of Contemporary Art*, accessed on June 10, 2018. www.jca-online.com/christo.html.

In 1962, Christo and Jeanne-Claude again took their work to the city streets. They illegally closed off a narrow Paris street, Rue Visconti, for 8 hours using 240 oil barrels to build a barricade. This work, *Wall of Oil Barrels—Iron Curtain*, was meant to protest the Berlin Wall, or Iron Curtain, that the Soviet Union had built in East Germany to prevent citizens of Communist Eastern Europe from migrating to democratic Western Europe. Having recently escaped from Communism, from his native land of Bulgaria to Prague and then finally to the noncommunist city of Vienna in Austria, Christo wanted to make a social statement. He wanted to draw attention to the restrictions Soviets imposed upon the citizens of Communist countries. Although Rue Visconti is little more than 12 feet (3.7 m) wide, it was an important thoroughfare, and the art piece created a traffic jam that tied up movement for 3 hours.

Mystery and Wonder

In 1964, Christo and Jeanne-Claude moved with their son Cyril to New York City. Here the artists took the wrapping idea one step further. The artists built sculptures that looked like storefronts and draped them with fabric or brown wrapping paper, giving this everyday object an air of mystery and wonder.

The scale of the works of Christo and Jeanne-Claude continued to grow until they achieved epic proportions in 1968. The husband-wife team created what they called "temporary monuments." Jeanne-Claude wrapped a three-story medieval tower and a baroque fountain in Spoleto, Italy, with woven polypropylene (a type of plastic) fabric and ropes. Meanwhile, Christo was working in Bern, Switzerland, on the couple's first example of a fully wrapped building. He wrapped the Kunsthalle, an art museum, in clear polyethylene (a common type of plastic). Commenting on another example of the project, the late art critic and journalist David Bourdon wrote,

If any building ever needed wrapping, it was Chicago's Museum of Contemporary Art, a banal, one story edifice ... having about as much architectural charm as an old shoe box ... Christo and Jeanne-Claude considered the building "perfect," because "it looks like a package already, very anonymous."[38]

The large projects were met with equal praise and scorn. However, the artists

continued to imagine works of art on a grand scale regardless of the reactions. Each new project brought new difficulties that required long periods to solve. For example, in 1971, Christo and Jeanne-Claude first dreamed of wrapping the former German parliament building, the Reichstag. However, the project took around 25 years to come to fruition. During the two and a half decades it took to plan *Wrapped Reichstag*, Christo and Jeanne-Claude attended countless zoning board hearings, public forums, parliamentary debates, public and private meetings, legal and contract negotiations, press conferences, materials tests, and

Wrapped Reichstag *took artists Christo and Jeanne-Claude many years to plan and complete. Five million visitors saw it before it was taken down.*

exhibitions. Hundreds of drawings and sketches were required as well as enormous effort and teamwork for the actual installation.

After the project was finally approved in 1994, the artists worked with 10 German companies that employed manufacturers, iron workers, engineers, environmentalists, and construction workers. Finally, in June 1995, Christo and Jeanne-Claude, accompanied by 100 German mountain climbers, wrapped the Reichstag.

Wrapped Reichstag was finished on June 24, 1995. More than 600,000 people came to view it the first day, and a total of 5 million visitors came to view the work while it stood. The wrapping came off 14 days later, as scheduled, and all the materials were recycled. As with all their projects, the artists refused to accept commercial sponsors. The total cost of *Wrapped Reichstag* was self-financed through the sale of drawings, collages, scale models, and early works of the 1950s and 1960s.

Wrapped Reichstag had special significance for Christo. The Berlin Wall had fallen in 1989, and East and West Germany were reunited for the first time since World War II. Christo commented: "The artwork … expresses freedom, poetic freedom—all projects are about freedom. This project cannot be bought or sold, nobody can charge, can sell tickets. Freedom is the enemy of possession."[39]

Yoko Ono's Instruction Pieces

The grand scale at which Christo and Jeanne-Claude's projects were executed was unusual for Conceptual art. Others created works that existed only as words printed on a page that were meant to evoke concepts in the minds of readers. For example, the 1964 book *Grapefruit: A Book of Instructions and Drawings* by Japanese-born artist Yoko Ono is filled with instructions. In *Hide-and-Seek Piece*, Ono wrote, "Hide until everybody goes home. Hide until everybody forgets about you. Hide until everybody dies."[40]

Grapefruit was an extension of Ono's so-called instruction pieces. These were intended to free people's minds and allow them to focus on their own creativity. In the piece *Painting to Be Constructed in Your Head*, Ono instructed readers: "Go on transforming a square canvas in your head until it becomes a circle. Pick out any shape in the process and pin up or place on the canvas an object, a smell, a sound, or a colour that came to mind in association with the shape."[41] To create *Painting for the Skies*, readers were told, "Drill a hole in the sky. Cut out a paper the same size as the hole. Burn the paper. The sky should be pure blue."[42]

While much of Ono's work was whimsical, some of her pieces were inspired by horrors she witnessed as

Harmony in a Warlike World

In 1968, Yoko Ono spoke to Tony Elliot from *Time Out* magazine. During the interview, Ono explained that the objective of her art was not to shock people, but to create unity and harmony in a warlike world:

People think that I'm doing something shocking and ask me if I'm trying to shock people. The most shocking thing to me is that people have war, fight with each other and moreover take it for granted. The kind of thing I'm doing is almost too simple. I'm not interested in being unique or different. Everyone is different ... The problem is not how to become different or unique, but how to share an experience, how to be the same almost, how to communicate.

Basically I am interested in communication and therefore participation of everybody. I'm just part of the participation ...

All my pieces are white because I think that white is the only colour that allows imaginary colour to be put on. In the Lisson Gallery I'm going to have a one room environment that's called "The Blue Room Event." The room is completely white and you're supposed to stay in the room until it becomes blue ...

So what I'm trying to do is make something happen by throwing a pebble into the water and creating ripples. It's like starting a good motion. I don't want to control the ripples and everything.[1]

1. Quoted in "1968 Interview with Tony Elliot, from *Time Out* Magazine," University of Wolverhampton, accessed on June 10, 2018. pers-www.wlv.ac.uk/%7Efa1871/yoko.html.

a child growing up in Japan during World War II. She was only 12 when Tokyo was firebombed by the United States and the cities of Hiroshima and Nagasaki were incinerated by nuclear bombs. In her Conceptual artwork, she tried to convey the loneliness of a child during war using art and performance.

One of Ono's most notorious works was based on her wartime experiences. In the 1964 performance *Cut Piece*, Ono dressed in a suit and sat motionless on a stage. She invited members of the audience to cut away pieces of cloth until, after about 40 minutes, she was naked, her mask-like face cold and unemotional. When explaining the meaning of *Cut Piece*, Ono said she wanted to express the isolation remembered from her childhood. She wanted the participants

This photograph shows Conceptual artist Yoko Ono in 2003 performing Cut Piece with her son, Sean Lennon. The performance was a repeat of the one she performed almost 40 years earlier.

to "hear the kind of sounds that you hear in silence ... to feel the environment and tension and people's vibrations ... the sound of fear and of darkness."[43]

Not all of Ono's work was so negative, however. She often used Conceptual art as a way of evoking positive feelings and affirming the power of imagination. In 1966, Ono held a show called *Unfinished Paintings and Objects* at the Indica Gallery in London. For this show, Ono used found objects that were either transparent or painted white, shades meant to convey peace. For example, *White Chess Set* was a standard chess set, but since the board and all the pieces were white, the game, which symbolizes a battle, could not be played in the traditional manner.

John Lennon, a member of the Beatles, attended this show and participated in one of the art pieces. He climbed a white ladder set in place to allow viewers to look at a piece of paper attached to the ceiling. Using a magnifying glass provided by Ono, Lennon read the tiny word "YES" written on the paper.

Other instruction pieces in the show encouraged visitor participation, a symbolic way of sharing the art with everyone. For example, *Painting to Hammer a Nail* consisted of a white panel, a hammer, and a jar of nails. A card instructed viewers to pound nails into the

Shown here are Yoko Ono and the Beatles' John Lennon. Their peace campaign protested the Vietnam War.

panel. *Add Color Painting* consisted of a wood panel, brushes, and paints, provided so patrons could add their own concepts to the work.

After Lennon attended *Unfinished Paintings and Objects*, he and Ono became inseparable. They were married in 1969, and Ono and Lennon then conducted a campaign for peace based on Conceptual art. In December 1969, as the Vietnam War was raging, Lennon and Ono published the message, "WAR IS OVER! / IF YOU WANT IT / Happy Christmas from John & Yoko."[44] This message was placed on billboards (with appropriate translations) in Hong Kong, China; London; Tokyo; New York City, and other cities throughout the world. It was also included in the Lennon song "Happy Xmas (War Is Over)" and distributed on posters, postcards, handbills, and in newspaper advertisements and radio ads.

A Lasting Impact

Christo, Jeanne-Claude, and Ono were among the few Conceptualists who were able and willing to speak to a wide audience. Most Conceptual artists rejected the art market, declined to create art objects to sell, and labored in obscurity. This made it difficult for the Conceptual art movement to hold together. Still, Conceptual art has had an important impact on postmodern art. Many postmodernist styles that followed oriented the viewer by having the artist provide some kind of context through instructions, notions, or language in the piece itself.

CHAPTER THREE

The Full Experience

nstallation artists often load gallery spaces with dissimilar, unrelated, and obscure items. Rather than create harmony, these combinations of painting, sculpture, poem, prose, and nonart materials are meant to evoke complex emotions such as puzzlement, longing, wistfulness, sadness, elation, or even anger. These "Environments," as they are sometimes called, may take up the entire gallery space and require viewers to move through them. An installation may also be set up in a way that requires it to be viewed from a distance or by walking around it in order to observe the piece from all angles.

As in Conceptual art, the concept or idea of the installation might be more important than the actual materials that make up the exhibit. While the viewer might react to the art in a certain way, he or she might not understand what the artist is trying to say. Museum curator Mark Rosenthal explained in *Understanding Installation Art*: "The [goal] of the modern installation artist … [is] how to reflect the experience of life—its complex issues, aspects, and appearances. The technique of installation has proved to be a useful tool by which to … speak about and investigate life."[45]

Like Conceptual artists, installation artists also attempt to redefine art, the artist, the exhibition space, and the art market. Before postmodern art, paintings had typically been framed and hung. Sculptures had been displayed on pedestals. Patrons stood behind velvet ropes or lines drawn on the floor so as not to intrude upon the seemingly sacred space surrounding the artwork. Installation art, however, attempted to get viewers to interact with the art, whether physically or spatially. Unlike exhibits of the past in which pieces were meant to be viewed individually, Installation art creates a collective experience for the viewer.

Patrons visiting an installation enter a room or space that is a surrounding artistic environment of sights, sounds, and even smells. They wander between different aspects of this environment, sometimes walking upon it, kicking it, or rearranging it. Computers, boom boxes, and video players invite viewers to push buttons, dance, or otherwise participate in the artistic space created by the installation.

Installation art is different from traditional art in that it takes place in time and space. A conventional painting or sculpture freezes a moment in time—and might be understood with only a few moments' study. The installation space, on the other hand, may occupy a viewer's attention for many minutes or even hours. According to installation artist Ilya Kabakov, "The main actor in the total installation, the main [center] toward which everything is addressed, for which everything is intended, is the viewer."[46]

Allan Kaprow

The postmodern roots of installation art may be traced to the late 1950s when American painter, performer, and Conceptual artist Allan Kaprow invented what he called "Environments." Kaprow considered New York's high-priced galleries, filled with sterile white walls, barren and uninspiring—places that were meant to be looked at but not touched. He wished to make art in places that were "'organic', 'fertile', and 'even dirty.'"[47] Therefore, Kaprow chose empty lots, dirty lofts, closed shops, abandoned buildings, and church basements to create his environments.

Kaprow's first event, *18 Happenings in 6 Parts*, took place in 1959 in three rooms of the Reuben Gallery that had been outfitted with clear plastic walls. An orchestra played with toy instruments while photographic slides were projected on one wall. Performers walked through the rooms reading from books or moving their arms at odd angles choreographed like dance moves. Meanwhile, an artist painted a canvas, pausing to light matches while a woman stood nearby squeezing an orange. Visitors were given tickets that directed them to sit in specific rooms for a particular length of time then move on to another aspect of the installation.

Artists Robert Rauschenberg and Jasper Johns participated in the event, which helped Kaprow get good

Words

I n 1962, Allan Kaprow held a "happening" called *Words* at a New York gallery. The event was described by Jeff Kelley in *Childsplay: The Art of Allan Kaprow*:

Kaprow divided the gallery space, which was inside an apartment, into two rooms. [In the] first, outer room ... hundreds of strips of paper, each containing a single hand-written word, were stapled onto the other two walls; here, visitors were encouraged to tear off the strips and replace them with others that had been nailed to a central post. All the words on cloth and paper had been randomly gathered from "poetry books, newspapers, comic magazines, the telephone book, popular love stories," and so forth. Crudely lettered overhead signs urged visitors to "staple word strips," "play," "tear off new words from post and staple them up," and "make new poems," among other actions ... Another sign, "lissen here hear records," directed visitors to three record players, on which recordings of lectures, shouts, advertisements, nonsensical ramblings, and so forth could be played simultaneously.

The smaller, inner room, maybe eight feet square, was painted blue and illuminated by a lone light bulb. Overhead was a black plastic sheet, creating a false ceiling that made the dark room seem like a graffiti space, recalling alleys and public toilets ... Hanging from slits in the plastic ceiling were torn strips of cloth, and clipped onto these were many small pieces of paper with handwritten notes. Near the entrance, paper, clips, and pencils were provided for visitors to add their own notes.[1]

1. Jeff Kelley, *Childsplay: The Art of Allan Kaprow*. Berkeley, CA: University of California Press, 2004, p. 71.

reviews from the art press. In the years that followed, Kaprow's events were eagerly sought out by New York's trendiest art followers but were often difficult to find since they were staged in odd, out-of-the-way places.

Kaprow's *18 Happenings in 6 Parts* helped coin the now-famous term "happening." Although the artist originally used it to indicate a rehearsed, strictly choreographed production, the word has come to mean a spontaneous, undirected event. While this was not Kaprow's original intent, his later happenings did become less structured.

For example, in the 1960 happening *Apple Shrine*, Kaprow filled a long, narrow room in a church basement with a maze of chicken wire, colored lights, bunched-up newspaper, straw, cloth, fake and real apples, and piles of garbage. The result was a very claustrophobic, or closed in, atmosphere. It smelled like fresh apples, which rolled on the floor and were crushed by the feet of visitors. Kaprow stated that he created the piece to draw attention to everyday environments generally ignored by people who live in them:

> [We] must become preoccupied with and even dazzled by the space and objects of our everyday life, either our bodies, clothes, rooms, or, if need be, the vastness of Forty-second Street ... [We] shall utilize the specific substances of sight, sound, movement, people, odours, touch. Objects of every sort are materials for the new art: paint, chairs, food, electric and neon lights, smoke, water, old socks, a dog, movies, a thousand other things.[48]

Kaprow also wished to create tension, risk, excitement, and even fear during his happenings. For his next event, A Spring Happening in 1961, he surprised the audience with a large power mower and electric fan as they moved between parts of the artwork.

In September 1962, Kaprow's Words pioneered the postmodern concept of incorporating words and language into an art piece. The artist filled two small gallery rooms with hundreds of strips of paper containing random words. Visitors were encouraged to rearrange the words into sentences, poems, or nonsensical phrases, or add their own words to the displays. This happening was meant to draw attention to ways in which words assault the senses in an urban environment.

Making Womanhouse

In 1970, Women Artists in Revolution (WAR), one of the first New York collectives, not only provided support for women but also organized demonstrations for equality. For example, in 1971, WAR protested the annual exhibition at the Whitney Museum of American Art because only 8 of the 143 painters displayed there were women. The Whitney responded by increasing women's participation to 22 percent the following year. In the years that followed, "Feminism ... [became] the most powerful ... political force in the art world,"[49] according to the late art history professor Irving Sandler in Art of the Postmodern Era.

In 1970, California feminist Judy Chicago created the first college-level feminist art course at Fresno State College. Two years later, Chicago, Miriam Schapiro, and 21 students from the Fresno class created a major installation called Womanhouse. The artists took over an abandoned mansion in Hollywood and converted it into an installation. According to Schapiro, the exhibit was based on the "age-old female activity of home-making ... Womanhouse became the repository of the daydreams women

Judy Chicago led the feminist art movement in the early 1970s. She has been a respected artist, educator, and feminist for five decades.

have as they wash, bake, cook, sew, clean and iron their lives away."[50] In addition to art, the exhibit featured performances by the artists, which were documented in the film *Womanhouse* by Johanna Demetrakas.

Working with materials such as shower caps, nightgowns, women's underwear, laundry, and other typically feminine items, women transformed the cold, decrepit mansion. The rooms included Beth Bachenheimer's *Shoe Closet*, Judy Chicago's *Menstruation Bathroom*, Sherry Brody's *Lingerie Pillows*, Brody and Schapiro's *Doll's House*, and Faith Wilding's *Womb Room*. In a *New York Times* article from March 2018, Alix Strauss described *Womanhouse*:

> *There were mixed-media environments and performances. Familiar rooms—kitchen, bathroom, bedroom and dining room—were re-examined, and the idea of a woman as a "happy homemaker" was questioned. The exhibit prompted the participants and thousands of viewers to explore feminism through the relationship between art and social change, and the complex, often-misunderstood relationship between a woman, her home and domesticity.*[51]

In early 2018, these issues were examined once again in a new exhibit called *Women House*. After several months in Paris in 2017, the exhibit was moved to the National Museum of Women in the Arts in Washington State. Featuring sculpture, video, and photography by contemporary female artists, *Women House* further explored the role of women in the home.

Judy Chicago's Next Big Installation

Chicago's next collaborative installation project celebrated the accomplishments of women rather than the oppression many felt. Produced between 1974 and 1979, *The Dinner Party* was a huge banquet table in the shape of an equilateral triangle measuring 48 feet (14.6 m) on each side. There were 39 place settings on the table, each one representing a famous woman.

The Dinner Party was first exhibited at the San Francisco Museum of Modern Art on March 14, 1979, where approximately 100,000 people came to see it during the 3-month display. After its premiere, *The Dinner Party* toured for nine years across the United States, Canada, Scotland, England, Germany, and Australia and was viewed by more than a million people. In 2007, *The Dinner Party* was permanently installed in the Elizabeth A. Sackler Center for Feminist Art in the Brooklyn Museum in New York.

Each of the three sides of The Dinner Party *represents different periods in history. The work honors the contributions of women throughout history.*

Ann Hamilton's Social Commentary

The huge public interest in *The Dinner Party* proved that installation art was a valuable commodity for galleries and museums. Although the genre was founded as a reaction against commercialism, since the 1980s, installations have drawn large crowds to most major exhibitions. As art historian Claire Bishop wrote, exhibitors "came to rely increasingly on installation art as a way to create memorable, high-impact gestures within large exhibition spaces ... Installation art is ... capable of creating grand visual impact by addressing the whole space and generating striking photographic opportunities."[52]

Some art installations grew to gigantic proportions. In the early 1990s, Ohio-born artist Ann Hamilton became known for using large quantities of unusual materials to create installations in vast spaces. For the 1991 Spoleto Festival in Charleston, South Carolina, Hamilton created *indigo blue* by artfully arranging 14,000 pounds (6,350 kg) of used blue cotton work clothes in an empty [T]he work was conceived [to] "blue collar" workers, or [work]ers, since indigo is a plant [...] used to make blue dye. [...] were meant to represent [w]orkers, who spend their [...]g American prosperity, [for]gotten.

Hamilton's subsequent projects were meant to invoke thoughts of livestock commonly used for commodities or killed for food. To have maximum impact, the artist created the installations to upset the patron's sense of balance, sight, hearing, and smell. For *between taxonomy and communion*, Hamilton laid sheep fleeces upon the floor and covered them with sheets of glass that cracked when viewers walked over them. In *tropos*, the artist filled a 5,000-square-foot (464 sq m) factory space with horsehair colored from black to blonde, sewn in bundles. The uneven floor space created by the hair, which was taken from slaughtered horses, was difficult to walk through and filled the room with a pungent smell. In the center of the room, the artist sat alone at a metal desk, burning printed text in a book, line by line, using an engraving tool.

From the perimeter of the room, located outside the windows, patrons heard the murmur of a man struggling to speak in a garbled language. The slow speech had the effect of transforming the empty warehouse into an otherworldly mental space.

Distorting Perceptions

Hamilton used natural and found materials to manipulate the viewer's sensory experiences. Other installation artists use contrasts between dark and light to disorient and control the behavior of the public. To

Stimulating the Senses

T he installation work of Ann Hamilton is known for its ability to stimulate the senses of the viewer. A 1999 article in the *New York Times* described her piece *Myein* from the same year:

> She created several parts for "Myein," beginning with the veil of rippled glass, which spans the pavilion's 90-foot length and rises 18 feet from the ground to its pediment. Set seven feet from the entrance, the steel-and-glass wall will distort the view of the pavilion, making it something of a mirage.
>
> Inside, gallery walls will be covered in a Braille translation of passages from Charles Reznikoff's "Testimony: The United States 1885–1915," verse that he published in the 1960's recounting court cases involving random acts of violence. The fuchsia powder will slowly descend from the top of the gallery walls, dropped by an auger system normally used by bakeries and pharmaceutical companies to control the flow of ingredients. As time passes, the powder will accumulate around the white Braille dots, making them visible, yet still frustrating the viewer's ability to read what they say.
>
> Meanwhile, from invisible speakers, Ms. Hamilton's voice will whisper Lincoln's message about healing the schism caused by slavery. It, too, is indecipherable to casual visitors because she spells out his words letter by letter in international alphabet code (alpha, bravo, charlie, delta and so on).[1]

1. Judith H. Dobrzynski, "Art/Architecture; Representing America in a Language of Her Own," *New York Times*, May 30, 1999. www.nytimes.com/1999/05/30/arts/art-architecture-representing-america-in-a-language-of-her-own.html.

do so, the artists build environments that require patrons to walk through twisting, turning, and darkened or pitch-black corridors that block out the typically bright-white light of the museum. Such passageways often lead to installations where video monitors, lights, and mirrors greet the disoriented patrons.

Los Angeles–born artist James Turrell is widely known for his instal-lations, which enclose viewers in order to control their perception of light. The artist uses optical illusions to manipulate the viewer's senses. For example, when viewers entered the installation *Atlan* at the Art Tower Mito in Japan, they saw what appeared to be a deep-blue painting on the far wall. As their eyes adjusted to the darkness, the blue seemed to swell and change color. Often, when

Playing with Light

In 2017, actor and comedian Abbi Jacobson hosted a podcast about contemporary art. In one episode, Jacobson and the essayist Samantha Irby experienced *Meeting* by James Turrell. After discussing how weird the installation made the two women feel, the curator of MoMA PS1 Peter Eleey explained,

It does this very interesting sleight of hand that a lot of great art does. It takes something out of the world so that we can focus on it. But in James's case it actually just uses the world as it is. He's not actually taking something and sticking it on the wall. He's cutting a hole in the wall so that we have access to this thing that we otherwise don't think about.[1]

Actor and comedian Abbi Jacobson, known for her work on Comedy Central's Broad City, *also hosts a podcast about contemporary art called* A Piece of Work.

---

1. Abbi Jacobson and Samantha Irby, "#4: Samantha Irby Gets High on Light," *A Piece of Work*, podcast, July 19, 2017. www.wnycstudios.org/story/samantha-irby-gets-high-light-turrell-flavin.

viewers walked toward the blue for closer inspection, they reached out to touch what appeared to be a solid glowing panel. They were then startled to find that the large rectangle was actually an open window into another empty, light-filled room. The eyes continued to play tricks. Although the opposite wall of the blue room appeared close, when viewers reached through the window to touch it they found it was far away. According to *Art:21*, "This window in the wall is like a portal onto another world, providing a view of a limitless space like the ocean or a starless sky. The work's infinite view is ultimately the product of one's own sense perceptions, and the viewer becomes aware of his or her own beliefs and habits of looking."[53]

These light installations create a visual phenomenon known as the Ganzfeld effect. This disorienting effect occurs when the brain registers depth, color, surface, and brightness as a single sensation. The Ganzfeld effect creates a sort of blindness comparable to an arctic whiteout in which people cannot tell up from down.

When a Turrell installation creates the Ganzfeld effect, patrons are ensnared in a space where the walls, floor, and ceiling seem to be blurred or absent. This upsets their sense of balance. Bishop described how Turrell's installation *City of Arhirit* affected patrons at the Whitney Museum of American Art:

Turrell could not fully have anticipated the physical response elicited by this installation; without form for the eye to latch onto, visitors fell over, disoriented, and were unable to keep their balance; many had to crawl through the exhibition on their hands and knees in order to prevent themselves from being "lost in the light." … [Several visitors] brought lawsuits against Turrell after having fallen through what they perceived to be a solid wall, but which in fact was just the edge of a Ganzfeld.[54]

CHAPTER FOUR

"Stealing" Art

The late rock star David Bowie once said, "The only art I'll ever study is stuff that I can steal from."[55] Bowie was referencing how all of human creativity comes from somewhere outside the artist. He did not mean that he went out of his way to plagiarize, or pass off someone else's work as his own. He meant that nothing in the world is original.

In the world of postmodern art, the act of borrowing one creation and using it in a new way is called appropriation. The most famous early example of appropriation art is Marcel Duchamp's 1917 *Fountain*. Although the urinal was made by the Bedfordshire company, when Duchamp appropriated it, signed it, and displayed it as art,

he started a trend that continues to this day.

The Art of Appropriation

The term "appropriation art" did not come into common use until the early 1980s. At that time, Pennsylvania-born artist Sherrie Levine created controversy by directly appropriating pictures taken by famed photographer Walker Evans. The Evans photographs depicted poor white Alabama sharecroppers living in squalor during the Great Depression in the mid-1930s.

Levine reproduced the photographs directly from an Evans exhibition catalog. In 1981, she displayed them as her own work, without making any changes, at the Metro Pictures

Rock legend David Bowie was known for both his music and his artistic expression. By saying he was a thief, he acknowledged that the inspiration for art always comes from external sources.

This photograph of Lucille Burroughs was taken by photographer Walker Evans. Evans became popular for his depictions of hard times during the Great Depression.

gallery in New York at a show called "After Walker Evans." In true post-modernist fashion, Levine's concept became more important than the photos displayed.

In her artistic statement for "After Walker Evans," Levine claimed that all images created by photographers or painters are plagiarized. For example, Leonardo da Vinci did not create the woman portrayed in the *Mona Lisa*, he only copied, or appropriated, her image and immortalized it with paint. In the same way, Walker Evans

Reproducing Reproductions

In the early 1980s, Sherrie Levine reproduced photographed pictures taken by famed photographer Walker Evans and displayed them in a show called "After Walker Evans." By appropriating the photographs, Levine gave them a new meaning. In 2001, Michael Mandiberg scanned Levine's photographs and created the website AfterSherrieLevine.com. According to Mandiberg, the website is meant "as a comment on how we come to know information in this burgeoning digital age."[1] On AfterSherrieLevine.com, he wrote,

A lot of conceptual art is an inside joke, and a lot of these jokes are one-liners. This site (like Sherrie Levine's work itself) is no different. Conceptual art positions itself within cultural theory and art history in order to "make a point" yet this point is often esoteric, inaccessible, and without real philosophical depth. In part, AfterSherrieLevine.com is this one-liner art prank.[2]

Mandiberg further explained the inspiration behind AfterSherrieLevine.com:

By scanning [these] images, I am bringing her critique into the digital age: one is increasingly likely to see (Walker Evans') images on a computer screen, and not in a text book; similarly the tools of image production have shifted to digital media.

By distributing these images for free, like open source software ... I have taken a strong step towards creating an art object that has cultural value, but little or no economic value.[3]

1. Michael Mandiberg, "AfterSherrieLevine.com," AfterSherrieLevine.com, accessed on June 10, 2018. www.aftersherrielevine.com.
2. Michael Mandiberg, "Texts: Statements and One Act Plays," AfterSherrieLevine.com, accessed on June 10, 2018. www.aftersherrielevine.com/texts.html.
3. Michael Mandiberg, "Texts: Second Statement," AfterSherrieLevine.com, accessed on June 14, 2018. www.aftersherrielevine.com/statement2.html.

simply captured with a camera the faces and bodies of his subjects and the objects they placed around them in their homes. Levine commented on this concept: "We know that a picture is but a space in which a variety of images, none of them original, blend and clash. A picture is a tissue of quotations [thoughts expressed by others] drawn from innumerable centers of culture ... We can only imitate a gesture that is ... never original."[56]

By challenging the concept of originality, Levine also protested the idea of art as a product to be bought and sold. Other postmodern concepts concerning the exhibit are explored on the Metropolitan Museum of Art website: "The series, entitled After Walker Evans, became a landmark of postmodernism ... and an elegy [funeral dirge] on the death of modernism. Far from a high-concept cheap shot, Levine's works from this series tell the story of our perpetually dashed hopes to create meaning, the inability to recapture the past, and our own lost illusions."[57]

Stolen Advertisements

Richard Prince got his start rephotographing the work of others. However, instead of appropriating famous art photographs, Prince took possession of advertising images created to sell cigarettes, expensive watches, perfumes, and designer clothing. Prince did not often photograph the entire ad. His images capture a fragment of the original photo, giving the appropriated picture a new meaning. For example, the 1989 *Untitled (cowboy)* is a photo of a cowboy riding a galloping horse with a lasso in his hand. Taken from a Marlboro cigarette ad, the cowboy in the lower right corner of the photograph is surrounded by blurred clouds and sky.

Untitled (cowboy) is from Prince's best-known series of images, all of which were appropriated from Marlboro ads. The photos were meant to explore the idea of the cowboy as

an example of the rugged individual who represented the ideal American male. However, since such a man only existed in the fantasy worlds of ads and movies, Prince believed he could only be possessed through artificial creations: "The pictures I went after; STOLE, were too good to be true. They were about wishful thinking, secret desires and dreams, not only the public's but [my] own."[58]

Prince did not only appropriate single images. In the mid-1980s, he began to use what were called "gang formats," or multiple images on one page. Inspired by the word "gang," Prince stole images associated with large groups. These included photos of drag racers, heavy metal bands, surfers, and people from the Hell's Angels motorcycle gang. Commenting on these photos, taken from ads and magazine articles, curator Lisa Phillips stated that Prince's images are not only images of "teen delinquency and anti-social behavior—but of people living on their own terms."[59]

Prince has been sued by the creators of original images and criticized for stealing the work of others. However, in 2005, *Untitled (cowboy)* sold for more than $1.2 million, setting a record for the most expensive photo ever sold at auction.

Getting the Point Across

In the 1980s, many appropriation artists used less subtle means to make

A Shift in Worth

In 2003, writer and curator Mia Fineman wrote an article in *Slate* about Richard Prince and the artistic success he found by rephotographing cigarette ads:

> In 1983, [Prince] showed a group of photographs called "Cowboys," in which he re-photographed Marlboro cigarette ads, cropping out the text and blowing them up to nearly life-size. These heroic images of Madison Avenue cowboys perfectly embodied the screwy zeitgeist [spirit of the times] of the Reagan years: a B-movie cowboy for president and a pill-popping first lady whose political mantra was "Just Say No." The "Cowboy" ... appropriations were like projections from inside the vaults of the cultural unconscious.[1]

While academic supporters of postmodern artists viewed Prince's work as a critique of commodity culture and championed the shift away from high art, a few years later, they were surprised to find that the appropriated pictures were hanging in the homes of wealthy art collectors. The work accomplished exactly the opposite of what those critics had been lauding them for: The artworks were a tool to brand the artist Richard Prince.

Appropriation artist Richard Prince became successful after using images of cowboys featured in Marlboro ads, such as the one shown here on a California billboard from 1997.

1. Mia Fineman, "The Pleasure Principle: Richard Prince's Post-Pulp Art Takes a New Step," *Slate*, October 30, 2003. www.slate.com/id/2090475.

philosophical and political points. For example, New Jersey–born artist Barbara Kruger gained recognition by appropriating black-and-white photographs from magazines, cropping out a portion of the image, and crudely enlarging it to a massive size. The artist then layered messages over the photos.

Many of Kruger's themes focus on the politics of gender, race, sexuality, consumerism, and cultural stereotypes. While using simple short phrases, her messages have a visual punch because they are juxtaposed, or put side by side with, the contrasting images of the advertising photos. For example, in *Your Body Is a Battleground*, Kruger pictured a female model's face with the words

"Your body" pasted across the top of the photo, "is a" in the center, and "battleground" across the bottom. This 1989 work became famous after it was used on posters advertising a major pro-choice (people who believe a woman should have the right to choose to have an abortion) march in Washington, D.C.

Another famous Kruger piece, the 1990 *I Shop Therefore I Am*, was described by Monica Racic in *d/visible* magazine:

> The title of the piece, of course in white Futura lettering, is written in a red rectangle and held between the thumb and middle finger as though it were a credit card or some sort or identification.

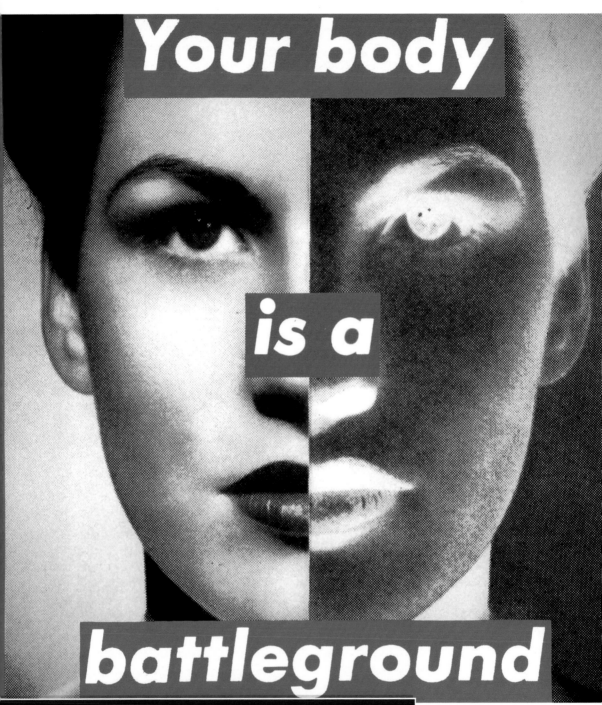

Your body

is a

battleground

Artist Barbara Kruger became known for her appropriated artworks, which focused on making social commentary.

The rapid reproduction of Barbara Kruger's I Shop Therefore I Am is ironic. In buying something that has the image on it, such as a tote, the buyer takes part in the commercialism Kruger is commenting on.

A *clear reference to [French philosopher René] Descartes "I think therefore I am," Kruger jokingly implies that in our society consumerism is valued and elevated to a level so high it supersedes consciousness. But on some levels could this be more than a joke? After all, a joke is usually half of the truth. Just think of the numbing effects advertising can have.*[60]

Perhaps ironically, Kruger's messages have been reproduced as typical advertising on matchbooks, billboards, T-shirts, television ads, and subway cars. They have also been exhibited in museums and public spaces around the world. By contrasting beauty, tragedy, humor, and politics, Kruger's work cuts through viewers' defenses and makes them take notice.

Legal Repercussions

While Kruger and Prince rephotographed advertisements, in the late 1990s, painter Damian Loeb skillfully used paint and brush to

Making a Statement

Barbara Kruger made a bold statement in 2018 when she covered the exterior of a building in Hollywood, California, with large, uppercase text. The building is the home of LAXART, a nonprofit exhibition space located on Santa Monica Boulevard. Kruger's work, *Untitled* (it), is a comment on the rising tensions between democracy and authoritarian power in the United States. *Los Angeles Times* art critic Christopher Knight described the work:

> When it comes to ordinary street signage for a pizzeria or muffler shop, we're used to something more playful or beguiling than "break it, own it, steal it, loan it, kiss it, slap it, hug it, hurt it ..."
>
> Holding up the abusive orders, the columns' white words on a black background sputter motivations: "pleasure, power, profit, property, poverty." Rising from beneath the windows across a podium painted vivid green, foundational words demand: "privatize, monetize, moralize, terrorize."
>
> Atop such base ultimatums, the "it" that is being broken, owned, stolen and hurt is unidentified. Instead, the object of the punishing verbal actions is neutralized; it is something less than human, not irreplaceable.[1]

1. Christopher Knight, "Artist Barbara Kruger Turns a Bland Building into a Screaming Statement. Time to Listen Up," *Los Angeles Times*, June 14, 2018. www.latimes.com/entertainment/arts/la-et-cm-barbara-kruger-laxart-review-20180614-htmlstory.html.

appropriate photographic images. These were recreated from found images pirated from art, newspaper clippings, fashion, and advertising. In 1998, Loeb produced controversy with *Sunlight Mildness*. The realistic painting shows four teenagers cruising in a convertible, an image directly appropriated from the photograph *Mijanou and Friends* by Lauren Greenfield. Loeb painted this image in the foreground of the work and juxtaposed it with a background image of a person shooting at a group of black Americans. Although the meaning of the original image was completely changed by the imagery in the background, Greenfield successfully sued Loeb and settled out of court for an undisclosed amount.

Although Loeb claims the settlement nearly bankrupted him, he continued to appropriate images for his work. Moving into the sphere of common cultural images, Loeb began creating paintings from movie stills he captured off DVDs.

In recent years, Loeb has moved away from image appropriation. His latest work features paintings of his own digital photographs that he has manipulated using a computer. Whatever the source, Loeb's images, which have been called photorealism, or hyperrealism, provide a view of manipulated reality that is both otherworldly and down to earth.

Appropriating Warhol's Style

Loeb's idea of lifting images from movies and ads was first popularized by Andy Warhol in the 1960s. Three decades later, New York–based artist Deborah Kass pirated Warhol's Pop Art style, bringing the concept full circle.

In 1992, Kass appropriated Warhol's silk screen style to explore her identity as a Jewish lesbian. The silk screen process involves burning a photographic image onto a framed screen. Ink or paint is poured into the screen and transferred to canvas, cloth, or paper with a squeegee.

Whereas Warhol silk-screened images of rock singer Elvis Presley, Kass created the *My Elvis* series. This consisted of multiple images of singer and actress Barbra Streisand dressed like a young man in the movie *Yentl*. Where Warhol screened Chairman Mao, Kass portrays Jewish lesbian author Gertrude Stein in pictures called *Chairman Ma*. Kass also gives

the Warhol screen-print treatment to herself, her grandmother, and *The Jewish Jackie*—a young Streisand in profile.

Kass was preoccupied with Warhol's style throughout the 1990s, and from 1999 to 2001, her traveling exhibition, "Deborah Kass, The Warhol Project," was seen in cities across the United States. Billing her work as "Feel Good Paintings for Feel Bad Times,"[61] Kass humorously explores gender, ethnicity, and sexual identity through her art. In doing so, she personalizes Warhol's style.

Hacker Artists

Cory Arcangel is unique among appropriation artists. Arcangel reprograms obsolete video game cartridges and computer software systems. He is among the few appropriators who call themselves hacker artists. As with so much other appropriation art, Andy Warhol makes an appearance in Arcangel's work as a pop-up cartoon image among a classic 1980s video game.

After viewing Arcangel's unique art at the 2004 Armory Show in New York City, critic John Haber wrote that the game "had the viewer's—no, make that the *player's*—eager involvement every step of the way. In more ways than one, it had all the right targets … It suggests a savvy, postadolescent hacker fondly recalling the technology and culture of his childhood. Nintendo and other early games are back ... as an unending cartoon road into a distant nowhere."[62]

Finding Inspiration Everywhere

Appropriation artists find their inspiration everywhere, but a society that focuses on commercialism and marketing certainly provides a fair share of fodder. The appropriation artists capitalized on what already existed in the world, and they used it with great effect to generate discussion and controversy. Highlighting the thought behind a piece of work is highly valued in postmodern art, and the appropriation artists used what was already present to make people think in new ways.

CHAPTER FIVE

A Return to Emotion

Neo-Expressionism, or "new expressionism," is based on the Expressionist movement that rose in northern Europe in the early 20th century. Norwegian painter Edvard Munch was one of the founders of Expressionism, and his 1893 painting *The Scream* is one of the movement's most famous examples. *The Scream* depicts a simply drawn, almost skeletal figure standing on a bridge with his mouth wide open and his hands covering his ears. The sky is a swirling turmoil of orange, red, blue, and aqua green. Although the figure appears to be screaming, he is actually in a panic to cover his ears so as not to hear what Munch described as "a great unending scream piercing through nature."[63]

Munch did most of his work in Berlin, and the pain, despair, and alienation depicted in *The Scream* inspired the school of German Expressionism. Like Munch, German Expressionists such as Ernst Ludwig Kirchner rendered figures in clashing colors with distorted forms and features. This slashing, fierce, emotional painting method was later adopted by Jackson Pollock and other founders of the Abstract Expressionist movement. Both the Expressionists and the Abstract Expressionists inspired Neo-Expressionism.

Neo-Expressionism was a reaction against appropriation, installations, and Conceptual art. The new wave of painters saw these forms of postmodernism as emotionless, cold, and

Edvard Munch's The Scream was inspiration for the Neo-Expressionists.

calculating, and they returned to painting forms that were easily recognized, such as the human body. Artistic skills with brush and paint were unimportant to those wishing to make political and cultural statements. Neo-Expressionism rose in popularity, according to critic Kay Larson, because artists were "desperate to reconnect with feeling."[64] These emotions were expressed through paintings that went against traditional composition and design, often portraying their subject matter in raw and rough ways using vivid color schemes.

Representing Human Emotions

Neo-Expressionist painters began portraying the human body and other recognizable objects in Europe in the early 1980s. In England, two important exhibitions featuring the new style of figurative painting were held at the Royal Academy in London. In 1981, the exhibition *A New Spirit in Painting* featured mostly German painters, as did *Zeitgeist* ("The Spirit of the Times"), which followed a year later. The 1981 exhibition was remarkable for two reasons. The display featured what curator Norman Rosenthal called "a manifesto and ... a reflection on the state of painting now."[65] It was also the first major exhibition of international contemporary painting anywhere in Europe since 1965.

The new paintings represented what Rosenthal called "human experiences ... people and their emotions, landscapes and still-lives."[66] Cocurator Christos M. Joachimides explained that the artists in the exhibition wanted to tell patrons about "personal relationships and personal worlds ... It is the need to talk about oneself, to express one's own desires and fears, to react to daily life ... to reactivate areas of experience that have long lain dormant."[67] This desire for personal expression through rough, violent painting would be the hallmark of Neo-Expressionism for the remainder of the decade.

Georg Baselitz, born near Dresden, Germany, in 1938, is considered a leading pioneer of German Neo-Expressionism. His style of depicting figures in a wild, brutal manner was undoubtedly inspired by personal events in his life. His first memories are of Nazism and coming of age under repressive East German Communism after World War II ended in 1945. His first paintings in 1964 were coarsely rendered depictions of what Sandler called "hulking, loutish peasants, herdsmen, and hunters ... all roaming the smoldering rubble of [postwar] Germany."[68]

In Bad Taste

By 1980, Baselitz had established his reputation, and exhibitions of his work appeared in cities across the globe. This created a hunger for

Baselitz is shown here with one of his paintings during a 2008 exhibition.

Neo-Expressionist paintings among American art consumers who were tired of the intellectual, introverted, abstract, and remote art of the 1970s. In New York, Neo-Expressionists Julian Schnabel, David Salle, and Jean-Michel Basquiat found their work in great demand. They were able to rise to prominence as a result of aggressive marketing by galleries and art dealers.

Schnabel burst upon the art world in 1979 with large paintings whose surfaces were covered with broken plates and jagged pieces of pottery. For the next two years, Schnabel painted figures with gruesome veins and scars on canvases littered with broken plates. According to Schnabel, "[The] 'sound of glass breaking or plates breaking' called to mind 'parents fighting or … screaming … The plates seemed to have a sound, the sound of every violent human tragedy … I wanted to make something that was exploding as much as I wanted to make something that was cohesive.'"[69]

Schnabel returned art to its most basic form of visual expression, and he quickly became the most talked-about artist in New York. In 1982 alone, he had 8 solo exhibitions and participated in 22 group showings. His paintings were selling for $71,000 in 1982 (which is the equivalent of more than $184,000 today), but he was widely criticized by art reviewers. As Robert Hughes wrote in *TIME*, "Schnabel is immensely fashionable with collectors for reasons the work does not make clear."[70]

Despite the criticism, Schnabel continued to depict figures in a controversial manner. In the 1983 *Vita*, the artist painted a nude woman on a cross. Art historian W. S. Di Piero described the

piece as formally "brilliant; conceptually, however, its presentation of the suffering female seems calculated to win sympathy (or approval) by virtue of its correct political tone."[71]

Schnabel began painting on black velvet. Once again, the artist gained notoriety for creating what some called bad art. Velvet is commonly used for garish portraits of 1950s rock singer Elvis Presley or tacky depictions of dogs playing cards. Some of Schnabel's subject matter—such as large portraits of his dog or obscene words—was also described as taboo and in bad taste.

Juxtaposed

The work of David Salle is often associated with Schnabel because the two painters are friends and found acclaim around the same time. Both artists paint in the Neo-Expressionist

Marketing Strategy

When Neo-Expressionists began to exhibit paintings in the early 1980s, they upset postmodernist purists. Critics believed the works of Schnabel and Salle were disreputable because of their commercial value to galleries, museums, and collectors. While some believed that the Neo-Expressionists had "sold out" for a profit, curator Diego Cortez defended the work both for its commercial value and its artistic worth:

> [Despite] its layers of materialism, opportunism, and ambition, [the market supports] the most significant art of this time. To the critics who feel this new painting is mere marketing strategy, let me say that they are only partially correct. It is good marketing [combined] with the best art … My admiration and respect for the new dealers who have supposedly "manipulated" and "packaged" this new art … is at least equal to that of the artists and their work.[1]

1. Quoted in Irving Sandler, *Art of the Postmodern Era: From the Late 1960s to the Early 1990s*. Boulder, CO: Westview Press, 1998.

style; however, their work is very different. Schnabel is known for heroic, biblical, and classical imagery. Salle's figures are often appropriated from photographs. These are culled from a variety of sources, including his own black-and-white pictures, news photos, cartoon characters, magazines, ads from the 1950s, and "how to draw" manuals. These images, gathered together on a single canvas and placed in separate rectangular boxes, are often unrelated. For example, the 1985 *Muscular Paper* consists of three large panels. On the left panel is a depiction of a photo of an abstract sculpture by Pablo Picasso. The center panel shows two females skipping rope, sketched in charcoal.

Meanwhile, two faces copied from a Jusepe de Ribera painting are featured in the center of this panel (a technique called overpainting). An orange lemon squeezer is painted between and over these images. The right panel consists of a piece of blue and green plaid material overlaid with an image pirated from a 1922 painting titled *Iron Bridge (View of Frankfurt)* by Max Beckmann. This image is said to be a tribute to the school of Die Brücke, or the Bridge painters, who were the founders of German Expressionism.

Muscular Paper and similar paintings reveal Salle as a master of juxtaposition, or the act of purposefully placing two things next to one

Shown here is the American artist David Salle, known for his juxtaposition of images that do not necessarily seem to go together.

another. He says he uses this method because he is unable to commit to a single subject, and multiple images can be used the same way a composer uses many notes to create chords in a song.

Many of Salle's critics do not see his paintings this way. Some are puzzled because the images are unrelated and arbitrary and therefore represent nothing. Others have accused Salle of sexism for how women are used in his artwork. Salle has responded by pointing out that his paintings, in some ways, resemble television commercials where models might be juxtaposed with images of pickup trucks. Therefore, Salle's fragmented images offer a commentary on the postmodern world that capitalizes on primal urges in order to sell products.

The Art of Basquiat

Few painters of the era could match the emotional impact of Jean-Michel Basquiat, whose primitive images flowed fast and furious as the painter rocketed to international stardom.

Basquiat did not attend art school, but rather honed his craft as a graffiti artist on the streets of Brooklyn, New York. Born in 1960 to a Haitian father and an

Jean-Michel Basquiat skyrocketed to fame after he painted graffiti close to trendy art galleries.

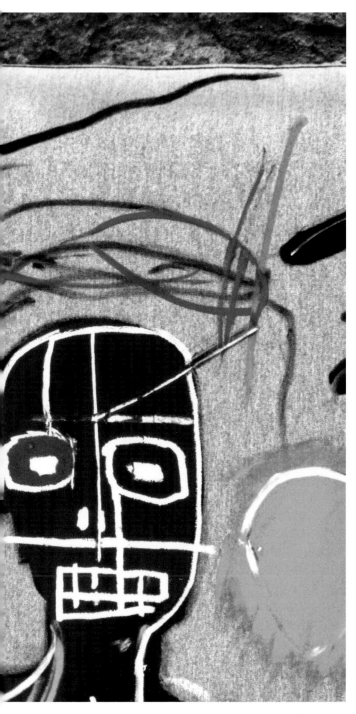

American-born Puerto Rican mother, Basquiat grew up in a middle-class home and strongly identified with African American and Afrocentric culture. He attracted attention with his partner Al Diaz, writing puzzling phrases on New York buildings and signing them "SAMO." His tags featured taunting lines such as "SAMO as a new art form. SAMO as an end to mindwash religion, nowhere politics and bogus philosophy ... SAMO as an end to playing art."[72]

According to the late art historian Robert Rosenblum, Basquiat was a "crazy kid from Brooklyn who began his meteoric career by raucously embracing a countercultural life, living in public parks, selling painted T-shirts on the street, [and] spraying graffiti on city walls."[73]

Although Basquiat's graffiti seemed randomly applied, it most often appeared near trendy art galleries in the SoHo district. By 1982, Basquiat had become a fixture on the SoHo art scene, playing in a "noise" band called Gray, which performed at punk clubs such as CBGB and the Mudd Club. During this time, he

Living and Dying the High Life

S everal weeks after Basquiat died at the age of 27 in August 1988, the *New York Times* ran the following article about his career, his life, and his death:

Some say he resented being a black man whose fate twisted with the whims of an all-white jury of artistic powers. Others say he pined for fame but was crushed by its burdens. Some friends believe greedy art dealers and collectors exploited him. Some say wealth fed his longtime appetite for drugs ...

Mr. Basquiat rapidly earned a reputation for high living. He staged lush parties with giant video screens and catered food, treated crowds to dinners at expensive restaurants, and flew friends to the West Coast for weekends. He painted in designer suits that were usually splattered with colors by the time a work was completed.

Much of the money also went to friends and strangers—Bowery bums to whom he gave $100 bills, and struggling artists who got free paints and canvas ...

Keith Haring, another graffiti artist who became successful, said Mr. Basquiat's extravagant spending on food and travel was his "way of sticking your nose up at people who were looking down on you."[1]

1. Michael Wines, "Jean Michel Basquiat: Hazards of Sudden Success and Fame," *New York Times*, August 27, 1988. www.nytimes.com/1988/08/27/arts/jean-michel-basquiat-hazards-of-sudden-success-and-fame.html.

was creating Neo-Expressionist paintings with scribbled words and graffiti, images from his life, pop culture references, and scenes from black and Hispanic history.

It was after a 1980 show in an alternative Lower East Side gallery that Basquiat was discovered by an art agent who brought him nearly instant success. The 20-year-old artist's highly marketable style attacked middle-class culture and was often painted on unusual media, such as broken refrigerators and other items retrieved from junkyards. Although Basquiat's images were anti-materialism and antiestablishment, according to Robert Knafo in an article for *Spike Magazine*, Basquiat "came to personify the art scene of the 80s, with its merging of youth culture, money, hype, excess, and self-destruction."[74] Basquiat used huge quantities of cocaine, used a garbage can lid for a paint palette, and often painted while dressed in expensive Armani suits, which he later wore in public, splattered with paint.

Basquiat's Afrocentric art was unique in the 1980s. As art curator Kellie Jones stated, "people weren't talking about Black or Latino cultures in the way [they do now]. In 1983 he was really ahead of his time."[75]

The crudely drawn 1982 work *CPRKR* (Charlie Parker), based on jazz saxophonist Charlie Parker, is typical of Basquiat's early style. The work, which resembles a tombstone, is painted on a piece of canvas tacked on tied wood supports. Brown paint is roughly smeared around the edges and the words "CPRKR STANHOPE HOTEL APRIL SECOND NINETEEN FIFTY THREE FIVE" are written on the work. (The word THREE is crossed out and replaced below with FIVE). This alludes to a memorial concert for Parker that occurred in April 1955 after Parker's death from a heroin overdose at the Stanhope on March 12, 1955.

An image of a crown appears beneath the letters CPRKR. Basquiat included the crown as a mark of respect, indicating that Parker was part of a royal family. The sax player is also referred to as Charles the First at the bottom. Other images appear to be blotted out with smears of black paint. Commenting on the work, Basquiat stated, "Since I was seventeen I thought I might be a star. I'd think about all my heroes, Charlie Parker, Jimi Hendrix ... I had

a romantic feeling about how these people became famous."[76]

By 1983, Basquiat had become world famous. He continued to explore his cultural heritage with epic works such as *The Nile*, which connects his own cultural heritage with the history of the United States and ancient Africa. *The Nile* depicts slave ships, and several African masks are painted on one side of the work. The phrase "el gran espectáculo" (the grand spectacle) stretches across the top, an ironic commentary on a shameful, centuries-long tragedy. Other imagery and words in the work allude to ancient Egypt, the early civilization along the Nile River that provided a basis of African American culture, according to the artist. Basquiat created many more monumental paintings that explored cultural identity and themes of justice in 1983, including *Notary* and *Undiscovered Genius of the Mississippi Delta*.

The young painter's talent and fame brought him to the attention of Andy Warhol, and the artists collaborated on several works. When Warhol died in 1987, Basquiat became extremely distraught, and his drug intake increased. Basquiat continued to paint, but critics became increasingly unkind, saying he was only repeating themes and images from his earlier works. On August 12, 1988, Basquiat died at the age of 27 from an overdose of heroin and cocaine. His last

Warhol and Basquiat became very close during the 1980s. When Warhol died after a routine gallbladder surgery, Basquiat became more reliant on drugs, which led to his death by an overdose in 1988.

painting, titled *Riding with Death*, is a simple drawing of a black and brown death figure riding a horse skeleton. The horse's skull has crosses in its eye sockets.

Basquiat's death made some in the art world question the ethics of an industry that could encourage a young man's self-destruction while profiting from his madness. However, even after his death, great sums were to be made. In 2002, Basquiat's sarcastically titled work *Profit I* was auctioned at New York's famous auction house Christie's for more than $5.5 million. The work was painted in Italy in 1982, when Basquiat was only 21 years old.

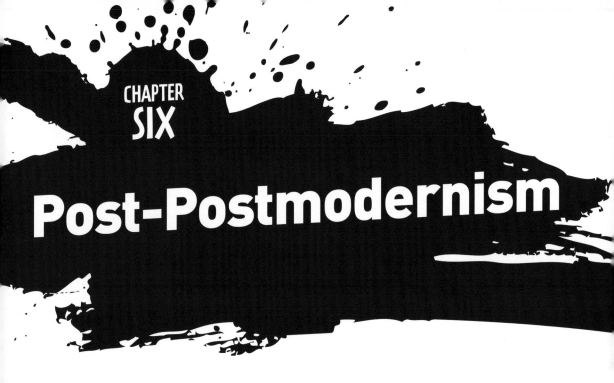

CHAPTER SIX

Post-Postmodernism

Just as postmodernism was hard to define at its beginnings, the end of postmodernism also has a vague timeline. Many critics refer to today as the digital age, which began with the rapid spread of the internet and new media technologies. Some critics believe postmodernism is dead, and they believe we have entered into a new era of post-postmodernism. Some critics believe the digital age will kill art. Indeed, some believe social media platforms such as Facebook and Snapchat and mass submission works have already killed art. After all, many people post clips of their everyday experiences all the time. Is that art or something else?

However, technology and the internet have made it easier for anybody to be an artist, and many artists today use social media as a way to spread their work. Many of the projects look very postmodern in theory. For example, in 2014 for $5,000, the Dutch artist Constant Dullaart purchased roughly 2.5 million fake Instagram followers. He distributed the followers to a group of artists in an attempt to level the playing field. Many would argue that power today is measured by the size of someone's following. As Dylan Kerr noted on the website artnet, "In a world that measures cultural capital by how widely your 'influence' extends (or seems to extend), fake followers represent a nearly socialist attempt at wealth redistribution."[77]

In fact, the internet has also done the work of getting rid of the middleman in the art market. Now, artists can post a photograph of their work or the work itself online and the audience can be connected to it right away. This effectively takes the art market out of the equation. While in the past, art museums and galleries had a large say in the artists who were commercially successful, now those institutions have little say.

Inspiration from Postmodernism

Even though the role of art in this new era has changed, what is certain is that artists will continue to take inspiration from what has come before and from what is happening in the world around them.

Postmodern ideas show up pretty regularly in the work of digital-era artists. For example, in *Steal Like an Artist*, artist and writer Austin Kleon argued that all art comes from other sources. He argued that great artists take the best ideas from multiple sources and mesh them together. "If we're free from the burden of trying to be completely original, we can stop trying to make something out of nothing, and we can embrace influence instead of running away from it."[78] This kind of thinking reflects the ideas of appropriation artists.

Kleon is known for blackout poetry. The artist uses a black marker on written text, and he shades out everything except for certain words, which remain and make a poem. Kleon is

Mayor rejects gr

Embattled Ford turns deaf ear
to party advisers, senior aides

**DANIEL DALE, ROBERT BENZIE
AND PAUL MOLONEY**
STAFF REPORTERS

Councillor Doug
Ford is "running
the show"
in the Ford camp,
says a senior
Tory source

Ford's   allies
call
the mayor

fight   er   a

a   lone wolf,

a   brawler,

warning   surrender could be

Mayor Rob For
Ford is seen he

political   defeat
Ford is
Ford

Co

Royso

is
Ford

ADVICE continued on GT2

ving chorus of advice

REUTERS

...ers are convinced he is a victim of a conspiracy among left-wing ideologues, writes Royson James.
...y leaving his mother's house with his chief of staff, Earl Provost.

...rvatives should dump Ford Nation

Possible mayoral candidates, such as John Tory, should cut Ford's followers adrift

...ticipated, a desperate Ford Nation is stopping ...hing to excuse Mayor Rob Ford's intolerable ...iour.

...r insisting for months that the mayor does not ...e crack and is being harassed by the "patholog- ...rs" at the Toronto Star who claim they saw a ...of him smoking wh... ...can't comment on ... ..., the whole fabricat... ...ce Chief Bill Blair a... ...a digital copy of the video on a hard drive of a ...uter seized in a celebrated drug bust that en-

snared the creators of the video.

Ford's cover blown, Ford Nation now claims they want the video released — the same video that they claimed did not exist; the same video Ford's buddy tried to retrieve with methods police now describe as extortion and for which they have charged Alexander "Sandro" Lisi with same.

This last desperate play springs from a strategy that says: Who knows what's in the pipe the mayor is smoking? You can't prove it's crack, so the mayor wasn't lying when he said he isn't a crack addict. Cute.

Ford Nation has a lot invested in Rob Ford. He is

JAMES continued on GT2

Shown here is a newspaper blackout poem created by writer and artist Austin Kleon. This style takes inspiration from Modern and postmodern artists.

also a good example of an artist who shares his work regularly through social media.

Appropriation in the Digital Age

Advanced digital technology has made art appropriation a much simpler process. Artist Benjamin Edwards uses that technology to appropriate the mundane imagery people are exposed to every time they drive down a busy street. In his earliest works, such as the 1996 *Gas and Fast Food Icons*, Edwards reproduced 36 business logos on two sheets of standard graph paper. He removed the company names, however. Viewers are left to figure out which icons belong to Shell, Exxon, Texaco, Pizza Hut, Burger King, Diary Queen, and so on. The work demonstrates how

Digital appropriation artist Benjamin Edwards uses his art, which features well-known business logos, such as the Shell gas station logo shown here, to comment on the increasing amount of mass media in our everyday lives.

recognizable these icons are without their identifying letters because they are such common images in the modern world. As Edwards wrote, most people are simply observers in a world that treats them as nothing more than passive shoppers and consumers:

> *Over the past several decades, the landscape has been transformed by the ... needs of the automobile ... [which] like television, a medium for advertising, [is] a funnel through pure consumption space. Travel through this space is cinematic, speed generating the projector: the colors, shapes, and images of signs, architecture, and billboards wash over and through the viewer. Through the frame of the windshield, landscapes, vistas, geometric compositions, and narratives unfold, approach, reach optimal visual display, then speed to peripheral view and recede into the rearview mirror to make way for the next presentation. The driver is a passive receiver, a screen onto which visuals are projected.*[79]

Edwards followed the icon work with the *Conglomerate* series, which includes dozens of wordless gas station logos layered upon one another. The most impressive painting of the series, also called *Conglomerate*, is a huge

6-foot by 9-foot (1.8 m by 2.7 m) canvas. The artist created it when he laid the building designs and logos from 45 national chain stores one upon the other. The painting seems to explode with the reds, yellows, oranges, blues, and greens associated with the distinctive designs of Borders (a former bookstore), Home Depot, McDonalds, and Starbucks. The look of *Conglomerate*, according to Simon Watson of artnet, is "an image of a single theme-park esthetic super-store, a utopia for euphoric consumerism where you can buy anything and everything."[80]

Edwards uses a laborious process to appropriate chain-store logos. He visits each store, photographs the inside and out, writes field notes, and makes dozens of drawings, called experiences, that include distinctive designs such as the red roof of a KFC.

Commenting on his inspiration for the unique paintings, Edwards wrote, "What will [the] capitalist vision look like in 100 years? In 1,000 years? I like to think of the world I'm trying to paint as one imagined from the eyes of an artist as far from our present situation as we are from ancient Rome."[81]

Asking Questions

Perhaps the most important takeaway from the postmodernist movement is the questioning of the idea of whether art is sacred. Postmodern artists stretched the concept of art as far as possible—so far that the importance of an artist or an artwork or even a critic was challenged.

If nothing is inherently important, there is room for questions. *What is beauty? Is art important? Why are certain aesthetics valued over others?* These questions allow people to take in experiences with more intention, and they allow for a more mindful approach to viewing the world. Even if postmodernism is over, the artists who challenged society's perception of the world have forever made their imprint, and their work will continue to inform people.

Notes

Introduction:
A Commentary on the Times

1. Quoted in Christoph Bode, "Manet, the Man who Invented Modernity," *Times Higher Education*, July 14, 2011. www.timeshighereducation. com/features/culture/ manet-the-man-who-invented-modernity/416799. article#survey-answer.

2. Irving Sandler, *Art of the Postmodern Era: From the Late 1960s to the Early 1990s*. Boulder, CO: Westview Press, 1998, p. 4.

3. "Postmodernism," Tate, accessed on April 28, 2018. www. tate.org.uk/art/art-terms/p/ postmodernism.

4. David Bates, "Beyond Postmodernism," LensCulture, 2005. www.lensculture.com/ bate1.html.

Chapter One:
From Modern to Postmodern

5. Quoted in Kristy Puchko, "15 Scandalous Facts About Duchamp's *Nude Descending a Staircase, No. 2*," Mental Floss, September 15, 2016. mentalfloss.com/ article/68674/15-scandalous-facts-about-duchamps-nude-descending-staircase-no-2.

6. Quoted in Jerry Saltz, "Cubes! The Horror!," *New York Magazine*, April 1, 2012. nymag.com/news/ features/scandals/marcel-duchamp-2012-4/.

7. Quoted in Thierry de Duve, *Pictorial Nominalism: On Marcel Duchamp's Passage From Painting to the Readymade*. Minneapolis, MN: University of Minnesota Press, 1991, p. 110.

8. Quoted in "Marcel Duchamp: *Bicycle Wheel*," MoMA, accessed on June 12, 2018. www.moma.org/collection/printable_view.php?object_id=81631.

9. Quoted in Jason Gaiger, ed., *Frameworks for Modern Art*. New Haven, CT: Yale University Press, 2003, p. 63.

10. Quoted in Paul Richard, "Marcel Duchamp's Museum in a Box," *Washington Post*, August 27, 1989. www.washingtonpost.com/archive/lifestyle/style/1989/08/27/marcel-duchamps-museum-in-a-box/e26b6954-0d71-4d6b-988d-9cfb342a0aee/?noredirect=on&utm_term=.4a584742e014.

11. Quoted in Alfred H. Barr, Jr., ed., *Picasso: Forty Years of His Art*. New York, NY: Museum of Modern Art, 1939, p. 9.

12. Quoted in Moderna Museet, "Exhibitions: Picasso/Duchamp," Moderna Museet, accessed on April 28, 2018. www.modernamuseet.se/stockholm/en/exhibitions/picassoduchamp/more-about-the-exhibition/.

13. Quoted in Moderna Museet, "Exhibitions: Picasso/Duchamp."

14. Quoted in Moderna Museet, "Exhibitions: Picasso/Duchamp."

15. Robert Fox, "Back to Futurism?," *Guardian*, February 20, 2009. www.theguardian.com/commentisfree/2009/feb/19/italy-art.

16. Leah Dickerman, *Dada: Zurich, Berlin, Hannover, Cologne, New York, Paris*. Washington, DC: National Gallery of Art, 2006, p. 7.

17. Quoted in Thomas McEvilley, *The Triumph of Anti-Art: Conceptual and Performance Art in the Formation of Post-Modernism*. Kingston, NY: McPherson & Company, 2005, p. 17.

18. Museum of Modern Art, "Jean (Hans) Arp: *Untitled (Collage with Squares Arranged according to the Laws of Chance)*, 1916–17," MoMA, accessed on June 3, 2018. www.moma.org/collection/browse_results.php?object_id=37013.

19. Quoted in Blake Gopnik, "D Is for Dada Making Sense of a Movement That Was All About Nonsense: A National Gallery Show Spells Out What Made It Tick," *Washington Post*, February 19, 2006. www.washingtonpost.com/archive/lifestyle/style/2006/02/19/d-is-for-dada-span-classbankheadmaking-sense-of-a-movement-that-was-all-about-nonsense-a-national-gallery-show-spells-

out-what-made-it-tickspan/
fb67be31-af0d-4934-9d05-
c93829df0387/?utm_
term=.90c8151f09ea.

20. Quoted in Elizabeth Fisher, "Art About Nothing," *National Review*, March 31, 2006. www.nationalreview.com/2006/03/art-about-nothing-elizabeth-fisher/.

21. Electro-Acoustic Music, "Dadaism," 2007. www.camil.music.uiuc.edu/Projects/EAM/Dadaism.html.

22. Quoted in Marjorie Perloff, "Dada Without Duchamp/Duchamp Without Dada: Avant-Garde Tradition and the Individual Talent," Electronic Poetry Center, 1998. writing.upenn.edu/epc/authors/perloff/dada.html.

23. Quoted in Juan Antonio Ramírez, *Duchamp: Love and Death, Even*. London, UK: Reaktion Books, 1998, p. 54.

24. "L.H.O.O.Q.," Marcel Duchamp.net, accessed on June 13, 2018. www.marcelduchamp.net/duchamp-artworks/page/2/.

25. Quoted in University of Exeter, "Where Dada Stands in History," 2007. www.spa.ex.ac.uk/drama/dada/page4.html.

26. Metropolitan Museum of Art, "Robert Rauschenberg Combines," The Met, accessed on June 3, 2018.

www.metmuseum.org/exhibitions/listings/2005/robert-rauschenberg/photo-gallery.

27. Quoted in "Jasper Johns: Ideas in Paint – About the Painter," *American Masters*, PBS, March 28, 2008. www.pbs.org/wnet/americanmasters/database/johns_j.html.

28. Quoted in "What Was Andy Warhol Thinking?," Tate, accessed on June 13, 2018. www.tate.org.uk/art/artists/andy-warhol-2121/what-was-andy-warhol-thinking.

29. Museum of Modern Art, "*Self-Portrait*, Andy Warhol," MoMA Learning, accessed on June 19, 2018. www.moma.org/learn/moma_learning/andy-warhol-self-portrait-1966.

Chapter Two: The Idea of the Work

30. Quoted in Michael Kimmelman, "Sol LeWitt, Master of Conceptualism, Dies at 78," *New York Times*, April 9, 2007. www.nytimes.com/2007/04/09/arts/design/09lewitt.html.

31. Quoted in Megan Gambino, "Ask an Expert: What Is the Difference Between Modern and Postmodern Art?," *Smithsonian*, September 22, 2011. www.smithsonianmag.com/arts-culture/ask-an-expert-what-is-the-difference-between-modern-and-postmodern-art-

87883230/#wZ3ejD2r0mUAq ZQ9.99.

32. Sol LeWitt, "Paragraphs on Conceptual Art," *Artforum*, June 1967. www.corner-college.com/udb/ cproVozeFxParagraphs_on_ Conceptual_Art._Sol_leWitt. pdf.

33. *Merriam Webster Learner's Dictionary*, s.v. "concept (n.)" accessed on June 19, 2018. learnersdictionary.com/ definition/concept.

34. Henry Flynt, "Henry Flynt's Concept Art," Radical Art, accessed on June 13, 2018. radicalart.info/concept/flynt. html.

35. Quoted in Gregory Battcock, ed., *Idea Art: A Critical Anthology*. New York, NY: Dutton, 1973, p. 176.

36. McEvilley, *Triumph of Anti-Art*, p. 65.

37. Quoted in McEvilley, *Triumph of Anti-Art*, p. 61.

38. Quoted in "Wrapped Museum of Contemporary Art and Wrapped Floor and Stairway," Christo and Jeanne-Claude, 2018. christojeanneclaude.net/ projects/wrapped-museum-of-contemporary-art-and-wrapped-floor-and-stairway?view=info.

39. Quoted in Werner Hammerstingl, "Christo's Reichstag," olinda.com, accessed on May 28, 2018. www.olinda.com/

ArtAndIdeas/lectures/christo. htm.

40. Quoted in Jonathan Cott, *Days That I'll Remember: Spending Time With John Lennon & Yoko Ono*. New York, NY: Doubleday, 2013.

41. Yoko Ono, "Painting to Be Constructed in Your Head (1) (1962)," a-i-u.net, accessed on June 10, 2018. www.a-i-u.net/ ono2.html.

42. Yoko Ono, "Painting for the Skies (1961)," a-i-u.net, accessed on June 10, 2018. www.a-i-u.net/ ono9.html.

43. Quoted in Jonathan Cott, *Back to a Shadow in the Night: Music Writings and Interviews, 1968-2001*. Milwaukee, WI: Hal Leonard, 2002, p. 258.

44. Quoted in HG Masters, "The Artist in Her Unfinished Avant-Garden," ArtAsiaPacific, May/ June 2008. artasiapacific.com/ Magazine/58/TheArtistInHer UnfinishedAvantGardenYoko Ono.

Chapter Three: The Full Experience

45. Mark Rosenthal, *Understanding Installation Art: From Duchamp to Holzer*. New York, NY: Prestel, 2003, pp. 26–27.

46. "Installation Art," Tate, accessed on June 20, 2018. www.tate.org. uk/art/art-terms/i/installation-art.

47. Quoted in Claire Bishop, *Installation Art: A Critical History*. New York, NY: Routledge, 2005, p. 23.
48. Quoted in Bishop, *Installation Art*, p. 23.
49. Sandler, *Art of the Postmodern Era*, p. 114.
50. Judy Chicago and Miriam Schapiro, "Womanhouse Catalog Essay," *Womanhouse*, accessed on June 14, 2018. www.womanhouse.net/statement/.
51. Alix Strauss, "Women, Art and the Houses They Built," *New York Times*, March 12, 2018. www.nytimes.com/2018/03/12/arts/design/women-house-judy-chicago.html.
52. Bishop, *Installation Art*, p. 82.
53. PBS, "Atlan," *Art:21*, 2007. www.pbs.org/art21/artists/turrell/card1.html.
54. Bishop, *Installation Art*, p. 87.

Chapter Four: "Stealing" Art

55. Quoted in Austin Kleon, *Steal Like an Artist: 10 Things Nobody Told You About Being Creative*. New York, NY: Workman Publishing, 2012, p. 6.
56. Quoted in Sandler, *Art of the Postmodern Era*, p. 386.
57. Metropolitan Museum of Art, "After Walker Evans: 2," The Met, accessed on June 10, 2018. www.metmuseum.org/toah/works-of-art/1995.266.2/.
58. Quoted in Sandler, *Art of the Postmodern Era*, PDF e-book.
59. Quoted in Sandler, *Art of the Postmodern Era*, PDF e-book.
60. Monica Racic, "You Are Not Yourself: A Glimpse into the Work of Barbara Kruger," *d/visible*, April 5, 2007. archive.li/lTi7Q.
61. Nikola Rukaj Gallery, "Deborah Kass," Nikola Rukaj Gallery, accessed on June 10, 2018. www.rukajgallery.com/deborah-kass/.
62. John Haber, "Cory Arcangel, Tim Hawkinson, and Charlotte Becket," haberarts.com, accessed on June 10, 2018. www.haberarts.com/boytoys.htm#arcangel.

Chapter Five: A Return to Emotion

63. Quoted in Tim Radford, "Stratospheric Echo Locates Munch's Scream," *Guardian*, December 10, 2003. arts.guardian.co.uk/news/story/0,11711,1103612,00.html.
64. Sandler, *Art of the Postmodern Era*, p. 223.
65. Quoted in Sandler, *Art of the Postmodern Era*, PDF e-book.
66. Quoted in Sandler, *Art of the Postmodern Era*, PDF e-book.
67. Quoted in Sandler, *Art of the Postmodern Era*, PDF e-book.

68. Sandler, *Art of the Postmodern Era*, p. 309.
69. Quoted in Sandler, *Art of the Postmodern Era*, p. 276.
70. Quoted in Suzi Gablik, "Julian Schnabel Paints a Portrait of God," *New Criterion*, January 1984. marshillaudio.org/downloads/Gablik%20-%20Art%20and%20God.pdf.
71. W. S. Di Piero, *Out of Eden: Essays on Modern Art*. Berkeley, CA: University of California Press, 1991, p. 209.
72. Quoted in Leonhard Emmerling, *Basquiat*. Köln, Germany: Taschen, 2003, p. 12.
73. Quoted in "Factory Work: Warhol, Wyeth, and Basquiat," Traditional Fine Arts Organization, Inc., 2006. www.tfaoi.com/aa/6aa/6aa349.htm.
74. Robert Knafo, "The Basquiat File," *Spike Magazine*, March 2, 1997. www.spikemagazine.com/0397basq.php.
75. Quoted in Tribe.net, "Jean-Michel Basquiat," February 18, 2006. afrolatindiaspora.tribe.net/thread/b26d10e0-7179-40b1-ae2f79cbbbf97c5c.
76. Phillips, "17: Property from the Estate of Jean-Michel Basquiat," Phillips, accessed on June 11, 2018. www.phillips.com/detail/JEAN-MICHEL-BASQUIAT/NY010717/17.

Chapter Six: Post-Postmodernism

77. Dylan Kerr, "'Like' Art: 7 Masterpieces of Social Media Art That Will Make It into the History Books," artnet news, December 20, 2017. news.artnet.com/art-world/best-social-media-art-1182398.
78. Austin Kleon, "15 Lessons from … *Steal Like an Artist*," Blockshelf, accessed on June 10, 2018. www.blockshelf.com/steal-like-an-artist/.
79. Benjamin Edwards, "The Rational Services the Romantic," Benjamin Edwards: Works, Projects, Archive, 1997. www.benjaminedwards.net/Writings/thesis2.htm.
80. Simon Watson, "Simon Says: Collect," artnet, September 24, 1999. www.artnet.com/magazine_pre2000/news/watson/watson9-24-99.asp.
81. Benjamin Edwards, "Biography," askART, accessed on June 15, 2018. www.askart.com/artist_bio/Benjamin_Edwards/11156924/Benjamin_Edwards.aspx.

For More Information

Books

Adamson, Glenn, and Jane Pavitt, eds. *Postmodernism: Style and Subversions, 1970–1990*. London, UK: V & A Publishing, 2011.
> This book explores postmodernism as not just a movement, but as an attitude that swept through the art world and then moved on to every other facet of modern life. With essays from a wide variety of critics and theorists, this is a good place to find information on the effects postmodernism had on society.

Bishop, Claire. *Installation Art: A Critical History*. London, UK: Tate, 2012.
> Bishop's work explores the idea of installation art, which she argues creates a space for the viewer to enter. It is a well-written history of the movement.

Emmerling, Leonhard. *Basquiat*. Köln, Germany: Taschen, 2015.
> This biography of the 1980s painter Jean-Michel Basquiat contains roughly 100 images, so readers can better understand the relationship of Basquiat's paintings to his life.

Paul, Christiane. *Digital Art*. London, UK: Thames & Hudson, 2015.
> Paul's well-researched book highlights many of the changes art has undergone since the creation of digital technologies and covers artists who have taken a lot of inspiration from postmodern artists, especially the Conceptual artists. This is a good resource for those who want to learn more about the direction in which art is moving.

Warhol, Andy. *The Andy Warhol Diaries*. Edited by Pat Hackett. New York, NY: Twelve, 2014.

> This is the 25th anniversary reprint edition of a collection of iconic Pop artist Andy Warhol's diary entries. As Warhol had something to say about everyone he met, this is a great resource for understanding both the artist and his time.

Websites

Christo and Jeanne-Claude
www.christojeanneclaude.net/

> This is the website of Christo and Jeanne-Claude, husband-wife Conceptual artists who are known for wrapping large buildings in fabric. Vistors can find updates on their latest works and information about complementary media, such as videos and virtual tours.

Deborah Kass
deborahkass.com/

> Deborah Kass is known for appropriating Andy Warhol's distinctive style, and information about her works can be found at this official website. It features upcoming events and artist statements on her work being shown today.

Imagine Peace
imaginepeace.com/

> Imagine Peace is the website of Yoko Ono, a prominent Conceptual artist still working today. It features blog posts and links to books, music, and events.

Judy Chicago
www.judychicago.com/

> This is the homepage of feminist installation artist Judy Chicago. Featuring her biography and recent updates from the artist and teacher, this is an excellent place for more information about her work.

Tate Gallery
www.tate.org.uk/

> The Tate is a Modern art museum located in London, England. The museum's website is a great place to find information about specific artists and their works.

Index

Picture Credits

About the Author

Amanda Vink is an author and actress based in Buffalo, New York. She has appeared in short films that have won international awards, and her written work includes textbooks, children's books, and the verse novel *And We Call It Love*. Amanda is also the fiction editor for the online literary magazine *Smirk*. When not acting or writing, Amanda enjoys hiking, spending time with dogs, and learning to play the bagpipes. She once toilet papered a public stairwell in the name of installation art.